MY JOURNEY HOME
LIFE LESSON DEVOTIONALS

DOUG CHATHAM

Mall Publishing, Co.

THE PRINTED WORD THE PLANTED SEED

NILES, ILLINOIS

Copyright © 2005 Doug Chatham

Printed in the United States of America

Published by:
Mall Publishing Company
5731 West Howard Street
Niles, Illinois 60714
877.203.2453

Book Design by Marlon B. Villadiego

Cover Design by Doug Chatham Jr.

Unless otherwise noted, all scripture quotations are from
the King James Version (KJV) of the Holy Bible.

ISBN 0-9760362-9-0

For licensing / copyright information, for additional copies
or for use in specialized settings contact:

Doug Chatham

2827 Janet Street
Lithia Springs, GA 30122
Phone: 770-745-2251
Email: drchat1@bellsouth.net

DEDICATION

This book is dedicated to my Lord Jesus Christ
and to my grandchildren who love him too:
Savannah Rose Mealer, Reed Malloy Chatham,
and Carmen Elizabeth Chatham.

TABLE OF CONTENTS

Part One

...

Some Old Testament Life Lessons

Part Two

...

Some New Testament Life Lessons

Part Three

...

More Life Experiences That Changed Me

INTRODUCTION

Book introductions often either synopsize the book itself or wax eloquent on the need for the book – I think the readers can do both well for themselves. In this case, the *messenger* is the message: I am choosing to introduce the author, Dr. Doug Chatham. Doug Chatham has been my friend for over a decade now. What began as a professional relationship between a college president and an adjunct instructor blossomed into a warm friendship. Since I am introducing a friend, may I call him "Doug" for the remainder of this page?

Doug is a mentor. He does it instinctively. It is intuitive for him. I know because he mentored me in so many ways. I want to be like Doug when I grow up. *Doug never meets a stranger.* I have observed him in literally hundreds of people interactions and I have yet to note anyone walk away without a piece of Doug with him. Yes, that's right. Doug has a way of planting his DNA in brief yet critical encounters. You know you've been with someone who loves God and His people. *Doug has forgotten more than I'll ever know.* Don't let his "aaaw, shucks...!" routine fool you. Doug is a brilliant scholar who has the awesome gift of taking the complex and making it simple without making you feel like a simpleton.

Doug is a perpetual learner, curious to know more. Anyone around Doug will notice how he lights up on new discoveries. That is why he instills a hunger and passion in all who sit at his feet. *Doug is a gentleman's model.* He is always respectful and congenial. Even in disagreements he is never disagreeable. *Doug is a leader.* He has incubated and birthed many churches and ministries here and internationally. He's really an entrepreneurial leader.

Doug is a visionary. When he came to me with the MOST idea (it's in the book), I was immediately taken by his vision and strategic plan to implement the vision. *Doug has attained significant personhood.* So many are trying to be successful. Doug has moved on from success to significant. His mere presence in a room is assuring due to his personhood. *Doug is contagious!* Yes, his infectious DNA is in you now. It's too late to get inoculated – you're being Chathamized! *Doug has more stories than Aesop.* Yet he will never bore you. He will make you cry and laugh simultaneously. Get ready… Chathamization has begun!

Samuel R. Chand, Chancellor
Beulah Heights Bible College

FOREWORD

Let me start with one of my favorite stories. Chippy was a highly talented canary. He could sing several recognizable popular tunes. In fact, a reporter wrote about him in the "Living" section of the Sunday newspaper. One day his owner was cleaning the bottom of the cage with a vacuum cleaner and was momentarily distracted when the phone rang. "Zurp!" Chippy was sucked down the tube! In shock, the lady quickly opened the canister and emptied all the dirt and grime out on the floor. There was Chippy, still alive but covered with filth. Quickly, she took him to the sink and doused him with cold water. Now he was clean, but wet and shivering. She grabbed a hair dryer and hit him with several blasts of hot air. That fluffed him back up, and she set him back on his perch. A few days later, the reporter called the lady and asked, "Is Chippy still with us?" To which she responded, "Yes, Chippy is still here, but Chippy doesn't sing much any more!" I sometimes tell this story to illustrate that unexpected events in life can make you stop singing. If that is the way it is with you, you probably don't hum or whistle much anymore either. Also, you may not smile or laugh very much now.

Life is filled with things you don't expect, and for which your preparedness is poor or none-existent. Most of us find our selves saying more than once, "I wish somebody had warned me about this!" Or, "I wish I could talk to someone who has been in my situation." What I share in this book are my own "life lessons." I have discovered over the years that there really is "nothing new under the sun." What happens has happened before. People around me are going through trials I have faced in the past. When I speak from experience and share what the Lord taught me in those times, it seems to help someone else. The devotional reflections contained in this book were birthed in my class devotional periods at Beulah Heights Bible College. Students have for years urged me to put them in print. As I began to collect and refine my notes, a realization dawned on me that these thoughts were mainly my own spiritual life lessons that God taught me in my personal journey. They really are quite autobiographical, since most of the spiritual lessons are illustrated with personal experiences. What you see here is largely a summary of those life experiences that have made me who I am. That is why I chose a title first suggested by my wife Jackie: "My Journey Home."

Most of what I have shared in the classroom was from the perspective of a mentor, one who has a passion for encouraging students to follow the call of Christ with their whole heart. It was always my purpose to show others the challenges and satisfactions of a higher calling. There is no cheap grace. If we would be made into useful men and women of God, we must be willing to pass through the refiner's fire. I am still in such a process even at this stage of my journey home. At age 66 I am sharing here some things an elder would tell any Christian disciple, but especially a younger minister.

Since this collection has evolved into something more than a devotional book, I have included a few reflections that were not originally given as devotions. I felt that the additional experiences would help provide for the reader a more comprehensive understanding of how the Potter has shaped this particular vessel. I also felt it would be useful to give you my personal testimony in Part One. I trust that each reader will find a personal blessing of inspiration and encouragement hidden somewhere among all these reflections.

I want to express my gratitude to Jackie, my sweetheart, mother of my children, and my ministry partner for 46 years and counting. If not for her encouragement to get started on this work, I might have procrastinated too long. Also, I wish to thank my children Douglas and Teresa for their patient perseverance and loving support through the trials which we experienced together as a family. What has shaped me has also shaped my wife and my children. And having them with me on the journey has helped me become something more than I could ever be without them. It is hard to even imagine what my life would have been like without Jackie as my pilgrimage partner. Douglas and Teresa helped their mom and me through many a rough spot with their good cheer, love and prayers. That support was particularly vital during an extremely difficult period when I suffered from Lupus.

Further, I wish to acknowledge my three precious grandchildren: Savannah, Reed and Carmen. Part of my motivation to set some of my more important life experiences in print has been my desire to have this as a means of sharing them not only with my grandchildren, but with other young Christians as well. Many of these memories and life lessons are also things a grandfather would say to his grandchildren. Perhaps there are other young Christian readers who would permit me to speak into their lives as a "spiritual grandfather." May this book be a blessing, and may God receive glory.

Doug Chatham
Christmas, 2004
Lithia Springs, Georgia

Part One
SOME OLD TESTAMENT
LIFE LESSONS

YOU CAN'T STAY HERE.

"And it came to pass, when they had brought them forth abroad, that he said, Escape for thy life; look not behind thee, neither stay thou in all the plain; escape to the mountain, lest thou be consumed." Gen. 19:17

"God has already shown you your next mountain."

God has delivered you. But you may have stopped too close to that from which you were delivered. You can't go back, and you can't stay where you are. If you do you will be eaten up. God's word to you is that you must climb the high mountain. God's call is an upward call – always upward. Higher standards, more difficult tasks, greater tests of faith. Lot first sought compromise. He settled for Zoar. But when he saw what happened to Sodom and Gomorrah and to his wife when she looked back, he moved higher. He left Zoar and dwelt in the mountain. The great lesson here is never to be satisfied with where you are. Comfort zones are dangerous. They can lull you into a false sense of satisfaction and cause you to miss your God-ordained destiny. You are here at this college because God destroyed your comfort zone. You are here because God showed you a pathway out of your past. But it's an uphill path. You have to graduate from this place of training – you may even have to go on up and graduate from a higher institution. God has shown you a mountain. Getting there may not be easy. But it is the only place for you. You know you cannot stay where you are. This will be a time of climbing.

In this Bible passage, the angel was warning Lot not to stay on the plain. He had to go higher. He had to get up on the mountain or he would perish. Sometimes the motive is to escape danger; at other times the motive is to gain some new level of understanding. That's what it was for Moses at Mt. Sinai, and for Elijah who later came to the same mountain. That's what it was for the three disciples on the Mount of Transfiguration. In a sense, a college can be a mountain that must be climbed.

I will never forget Saturday morning, February 27, 1993. That's when my wife and I left St. Catherine's Monastery and climbed up to the 7,400 feet level of Mount Sinai – the very top. By 7 AM we were there. But getting there was a miracle. We had forgotten how cold it gets in the higher elevations of the Sinai desert at night. We didn't take any warm clothes and had to hastily make layered outfits out of extra shirts and pants. My wife didn't have any good walking shoes, let alone mountain climbing shoes. And we were both totally out of shape.

So after the first half mile, I had to coax my wife around each upward hairpin turn in the rocky path. I had to keep convincing her we had come too far to turn back now. We could only see a few yards ahead with my tiny flashlight. The rest of the group had either gone on ahead or had dropped out and were now behind us. We were alone in the dark. So I would shine the light as far up the trail as it would reach, and it looked like we could do at least that much more before we quit. And then we would repeat the procedure. Each time I would say, "I think we're really close to the top. Let's climb a little more and see." We could only see the next few steps. And we knew we could make those. Then we could see a few more. And we knew we could get that far. We climbed near-ly a 1,000 feet over loose and slippery rocks and reached the summit just at sunrise.

What an awesome view! But we would never have reached the top if we had been able to see the whole tortuous way before we started. Eventually we were there. And the sunrise was spectacular. We were on the highest peak of the Horeb range. All those red mountains were glowing beneath us as though they were on fire. Off to our west a bank of clouds reflected the golden light of the sun. And in that eerie silence, we heard a small group of Korean pilgrims just beneath us singing "Alleluia." It was so fitting – for that moment for us in that awesome place.

I have often thought, what if we had decided we couldn't make it? We would have turned back and missed all this! That's the way it is with God's greatest blessings. You have to want to keep on climbing. It needs to be an attitude and a lifestyle. Attitude determines altitude. If you don't think you can climb any higher, then you won't. So if four years of study is your mountain, you will have to treat each semester like a new turn in the road upward, and just keep climbing. Remember, if you're not climbing, you're not gaining any alti-tude. Your work here will be like that. You know where you're heading. You have seen people graduate. You know it can be done. But for now you can't see every course, every assignment, every research paper, and every final exam. Just see the next assignment, and know with God's help you will get on up this mountain!

GET YOUR LIFE UNDER CONTROL.

"And the Lord said unto Moses, Put forth thine hand, and take it by the tail. And he put forth his hand, and caught it, and it became a rod in his hand:" Exodus 4:4

"When your life seems out of control, turn loose and let God take over."

I was driving along I-24 in Tennessee, going over a mountain called Monteagle. Suddenly a blinding rain hit the windshield, and the cars ahead threw on brakes. I did too, and the car started in a sideways skid – toward a rail and beyond it the edge of a cliff. I wrestled with the wheel, but we continued to skid toward the edge. I heard God say, "Let go." I took my hand off the wheel, and the car straightened up just in time. Afterward, as I reflected upon what had happened I realized that God had a purpose in allowing the near catastrophe to happen. I sought in prayer for understanding, and I learned a spiritual lesson. We aren't in charge. Life can very quickly go out of our control! Then we will have to learn to let go and let God take over.

Moses had to learn this lesson in the desert. His political career was shot. He was unable to do anything for his family and his people back in Egypt. He was just keeping sheep for his father-in law. Then at the burning bush, God got his attention and taught him a lesson. His shepherd's rod was a symbol of control. God told him to throw it down, and when he did it became a snake. Then God said pick it back up, but take it by the tail. When he did, it turned back into a rod, but from then on, it was known as the rod of God. Three things: One, release what you think you are in charge of. Two, don't take it back unto God tells you to do it. Three, never again take it by the head. Let God do that. That means you no longer make command decisions. You pray about direction, choice, and wisdom constantly. And you get your spirit in position to know the difference between a rod and a snake. This is a season of working on letting go and letting God.

It's really amusing to think how our efforts to be "in charge" must appear to God. We really are not in control of anything except our individual choices of how we will respond or react to those things which are beyond our control. It's like the husband who told everyone that he and his wife divided up all their household decisions "fifty-fifty." When pressed he admitted, "She makes all the big decisions and I make all the little ones." A senator who spoke at one of my Bless Israel rallies and I were chatting just before the program. I asked, "How are things in Washington?" He responded, "Well, Congress is like a bunch of ants on a log floating down the Potomac. Each one thinks he's driving!"

Let's learn to do as Moses did. Pick up the tail of every problem and let God have the head. It has been a blessing of greater peace in my life to realize I am not in charge, but my God is. I can lie down at night and not worry. I can get up in the morning without dread. People say to me in the midst of some personal crisis, "I don't know how you can stand it!" And I say, "How do I stand what?" God has brought me to a place where is no difference from one day to the next, regardless of the particular challenges I am facing. My credo is that my God is in charge. Is that the way it is with you? Pray that you can let go and let God!

MOVING WITH THE CLOUD

"And on the day that the tabernacle was reared up the cloud covered the tabernacle, namely, the tent of the testimony; and at even there was upon the tabernacle as it were the appearance of fire, until the morning. So it was always: the cloud covered it by day, and the appearance of fire by night. And when the cloud was taken up from the tabernacle, then after that the children of Israel journeyed: and in the place where the cloud abode, there the children of Israel pitched their tents. At the commandment of the LORD the children of Israel journeyed, and at the commandment of the LORD they pitched: as long as the cloud abode upon the tabernacle they rested in their tents. And when the cloud tarried long upon the tabernacle many days, then the children of Israel kept the charge of the LORD, and journeyed not. And so it was, when the cloud was a few days upon the tabernacle; according to the commandment of the LORD they abode in their tents, and according to the commandment of the LORD they journeyed." Numbers 9:15-20

"Never make a major move without divine direction. If you pray and don't get any new direction, have the good sense to just stay where you are!"

Understand the situation in this passage. Think about the harsh conditions of this wilderness journey. Think about how hard it would be to set up a campsite: brush for fire, water for animals and for cooking. Corrals for animals. Tents for shelter. Think about their desperate dependence upon God for everything: Manna from the sky, water to drink, direction to travel, protection from enemies. Now think about having to follow a cloud that kept you from burning up in the desert, and lighted your way at night. Never knowing if you would be at a place a month, or a week or only a day, or just part of one night? Can you be that flexible without complaining? How do you feel when you lose your comfort zone?

Here are some lessons. One: don't stay in your past when God signals a move in the present. Two: move only with the cloud (God's blessing and direction). Don't go in the wrong direction simply because that's where you want God to take you. Three: Don't outrun the cloud – don't try to have the future when he is providing only for the present. You may know where God wants you in the future, but you may not yet know *when* He wants you there. Four: Learn to be flexible, stay alert and sensitive to the cloud. I pastored some new works 9 months, and others 9 years. Be willing to move, but be willing to stay. I came to BHBC expecting to move on within a year. I'm still here after 12 years, because for me the cloud is still here.

I recall that early on in my ministry, I prayed for God to lead my wife Jackie and me to a place of service. He did, with circumstances which had His unmistakable fingerprints. In fact, it was so every time we moved. Each time, I hoped to settle down and grow old there. But there always came a time when I knew it was time to move on. In those first several moves, I would have been hard pressed to put in words exactly *how* I knew. I just knew. And it was not always just me. Sometimes Jackie knew first. Sometimes I knew first and had to try to explain it to her and the children. Now I realize that the knowing came from the Holy Spirit. But there were times when externally everything was still going well. People would ask, "Why would you want to go now?" My only answer was, "I just know it's time to go. God has something else for me now." And He always did. I urge you, dear reader, to make it your business to watch the cloud of God's presence. Always be ready to stay no matter what; ready to go no matter what!

WATCH WHAT YOU SAY!

"Say unto them, As truly as I live, saith the LORD, as ye

have spoken in mine ears, so will I do to you:" Numbers 14:28

"Out of your heart come the issues of life. What you inwardly focus upon will create the direction of the flow of your life."

Think about the background of this text. They had every-thing. And they blew it by holding on to a negative focus. They had just refused to go ahead into another phase of bless-ings, because it didn't make sense to their minds to go into Canaan at that time. They kept saying, "We're going to die in this desert, we're going to die in this desert." So God said, "As you have spoken in my ears, so shall it be." You will have what you say. Have you ever tried to get a child to do a chore or some homework - and all you get is, "I can't?" Do you know any fellow students here who have the same attitude? "I can't use a computer." "I can't write a paper." "I can't do all that reading." If they keep that attitude, they will be the drop-outs.

There are some great principles here. First: Life follows the direction of your focus. Be careful what you let your mind dwell on. If you constantly expect the worst, you are more apt to get it through such a negative mindset. This is true of the whole range of life situations: illnesses, job applications, mar-riages, child-rearing and even your performance in school. Secondly: Learn to think and speak only positive things. If you are hopeful and look for good things, you are more apt to have them. It helps to let others hear you put your good expecta-tions in words. Voicing your expectations becomes even more powerful when you base them on scriptural truth. Some good scriptures to read are: Isaiah 59:19; Matthew 12:34-37; Ecclesiastes 5:6; Proverbs 10:19; Colossians 4:6. Memorize these verses. Thirdly, lead the way for others in cutting a positive channel. Remember the Shunemite Woman in 2 Kings 4:26. She kept saying, "It shall be well." "It is well." And no matter how the story might have ended, that statement was absolutely true. Because her understanding of the situation was right, her confession was right and eventually it turned out all right.

Put these three great principles to work in your life. Start with a more positive focus. If you are constantly thinking negative thoughts, make up your mind that you will rebuke these thoughts as not from God's Holy Spirit. Instead, follow Paul's advice to the Philippians and only think on what is true and pure and good. Then make sure that you speak good things based on promises in God's Word. And learn to say, about any hard or difficult challenge, "It shall be well." In fact, try to move to greater faith and make the declaration that "It is well!" That's really true in the light of Romans 8:28. God is working all things together for good in your behalf. So, while you are here in this place of learning, learn to say, "It is well." Say it often. Say it about everything! You will find your faith growing daily, and you will see things turn out positively much more frequently. Try it and see!

FALSE FIRE IN MINISTRY

"And Nadab and Abihu, the sons of Aaron, took either of them his censer, and put fire therein and put incense thereon, and offered strange fire before the LORD, which he commanded them not. "And there went out fire from the LORD, and devoured them, and they died before the LORD. Then Moses said unto Aaron, This is it that the LORD spake, saying, I will be sanctified in them that come nigh to me, and before all the people I will be glorified. And Aaron held his peace." Leviticus 10: 1-3

"Don't ever try to pretend you have the fire when you don't."

This was the day when Nadab and Abihu had been ordained in an elaborate ceremony. Now they were being installed as priests. They apparently had gone out and celebrated with "strong drink" (vs. 9-11). God had instructed that at the time to offer the sacrifice, the priest would prepare the meat on the wood on the altar exactly as told.

Then God would show his approval by supernaturally kindling fire on the altar, without any help from man. This had just been demonstrated when Aaron offered a sacrifice. Now was their turn, and they waited and no fire came. They had indulged in drinking and gotten so intoxicated, they were not even aware of how supernatural worship is supposed to be. No fire came, so they just got some coals and started a fire of their own. God calls it "strange fire." But God did not accept it. In fact He judged it. He sent fire all right. But it burned them to death.

Here are some lessons that I have drawn from this passage: First, never offer false worship. Worship leader: If you don't feel it, pray until you do. If God's spirit doesn't light the fire as you step onto the platform, immediately back up and get on your knees. In the pew: if the words are not real to you, just close your eyes and lift your heart to God and don't sing or clap or do anything without putting your heart into it. Secondly, never offer God anything else that is false – like false giving and false tithing. If you give grudgingly, that's false fire. If you give something less than your tithe and call it a tithe, that's false fire. Thirdly, never offer false testimony. That's when the fire you produce is from your own story-telling and not from God's working through you. Are you trying to jazz it up and make it more impressive to others? Watch that. When you start lying in your testimony, you are offering false fire. Fourthly, never offer false preaching. Are you preaching to entertain? Or are you preaching so that the Holy Spirit will work on hearts and Jesus will be glorified?

What made this worship false? Read verses 3, 9, and 10. Ministers: guard against living and acting like the world around you. Stop treating your calling as a professional career. Stop treating your ministerial office like a membership in a country club with all those perks and privileges. Don't ever treat your speaking opportunities like a Toastmaster's Club event. Read verse 7 again. "for the anointing oil is upon you." Not just a slick liquid, but a true spiritual blessing from God.

Don't ever treat that lightly. Don't ever offer false fire. Maybe God won't actually send real fire to burn up someone who is using the pulpit falsely, but He will judge such a person in due time. I have seen ministers fall, and fall hard. Knowing some of them, had I been God I might have acted much more quickly. But our God is longsuffering and patient. Today in the age of grace, He gives us all plenty of time to see the error of our ways. But there are limits beyond which God will not permit false fire. Woe to anyone who keeps on pushing God toward that limit! Let's pray that our witness will always be real.

MAKING A NEW START

"Ye have compassed this mountain long enough: turn you northward. " Deuteronomy 2:3

"All effective ministries begin with a time of training – in the Word of God."

There are some powerful metaphors in this story. The Exodus from Egypt represents our salvation. Mt Sinai represents our covenant to learn and do the Word of God. The Wilderness represents our testing ground. Notice that this story involves all of God's people. It applies to whole congregations, to all real churches in a community, and to the Body of Christ worldwide. But it also applies to individuals: Moses, David, Jesus, Paul – all had their time in the wilderness before their public ministry.

Look at the lessons here: First, training is of no value if you are not delivered. Getting out of Egypt is the first priority. You should thank God that you have been saved and set free of old habits – old struggles – old relationships. Secondly, next comes training, and it must come before your time of testing in the Wilderness. So first you come to Mt. Sinai and you stay there until God says move. Billy Graham tells of a phase of his life when the girl to whom he was engaged broke it off because he didn't act like he would ever amount to anything. He was going back and forth on whether the Word was tampered with by man or whether it was all true. He finally came to a point where he committed to the conviction that the Word of God was all true, and he would live by it and preach that it was. Thirdly, then comes the launching out on your journey, the beginning of your testing time. This is your time the Wilderness. You could cut your time short if you would just learn to obey. But you will miss opportunities and make long detours. You may have to go around all sorts of mountains. But even that has an end. You can't and won't have to keep going around and around. One day you will hear a word from God: "You've gone around this mountain long enough."

But remember, you haven't done anything long enough until God says it's enough! You may feel that you've had it! You just can't go around in this familiar circle again – not a single step more. But if you try to make a move without God's direction and His peace in your heart, you will just get into a situation far worse. I sometimes tell the story of some cowboys rounding up stray cattle. In one ravine, they cornered a large bull. He charged the nearest cowboy. The others yelled, "Jump into that cave there." He did so as the bull thundered past. But he jumped back out too soon, and the bull started another charge. They yelled, "Stay in the cave!" He yelled back, "I can't! There's a bear in there!" So it will be with you if you move ahead of God's perfect timing. You will find a place all right, but it won't work for you!

But one day, there will come a time when God says you've gone around where you are long enough. When He does, you are going to make a new start, and this time you are going somewhere! But let me give a word of caution. Some people understand too well that you can't move until God releases you. But they are so afraid of making a mistake in the new move, that they just stay where they are – petrified with fear of the unknown. They then rationalize and explain to themselves that what they thought was God's voice telling them to move was just their own imagination. Then they waste precious years of their lives not moving when God says move. Pray for grace to be willing to move. You can even pray to be made willing to be willing!

While you are here at this college, you will get impatient. It will seem like you're just going around and around a mountain. But stay where God put you, and keep doing the job God gave you and until it is finished. When it is time, God will let you know. (Graduation will be a good clue)! Until then, learn to be faithful where you are. It's not long enough until God says it's long enough. You, dear reader, may not be in college but you can wholeheartedly identify with the idea of going around and around and seemingly getting nowhere. Keep your heart close to God and listen with your spirit. One day soon, you will hear Him say, "You've been going around this mountain long enough!" Until then, He gives grace for where He has put you.

RECOGNIZING WHEN IT'S A NEW SEASON

"Moses my servant is dead; now therefore arise, go over this Jordan, thou, and all this people, unto the land which I do give to them, even to the children of Israel." Joshua 1:2

"You may be about to cross a Jordan River in your life."

God was speaking to Joshua. He said, "Moses my servant is dead. Now therefore arise and go over this Jordan..." Moses' death was a turning point. Certain events in our lives have turned out to be pivotal points. Our lives changed. We started out in a new season. It is usually the case that something painful happens, as it did here in the death of Moses. But through the pain came a new beginning – a big change in our lives. That's how some of you got here to this school!

I have made some new starts in my spiritual journey. Leaving comfort zones to plant new churches with no financial support. Starting to college; starting to seminary. Starting missions overseas. Being re-comissioned as a teaching apostle. Coming here to teach. It turns out that these events opened up whole new seasons in my life. How do you know if you have embarked upon a new season? Is this a continuation of the way things have been? Or is it a whole new season – and you need to adjust to it? How do you know? In this passage we have some tests we can apply to your situation.

First, is the time of apprenticeship over? (verse 2) Not because you can't get along with your senior minister, or boss. Just simply the fact that he or she is no longer there. That's a good sign it's over. Moses was gone. Secondly, are you being given a new geographical location? (verses 2-3). Where you have been before was not really yours – but God has worked it out so that now you will have a place to settle down. Thirdly, are you experiencing new success? (verse 5) The opposition you would normally face has been taken out of the way. God promises that He will not fail you, nor forsake you! Fourthly, is this being accompanied by a stronger spiritual focus? (verses 7-8) That's how you know it's not the Devil just setting you up for a fall, or your own flesh nature leading you into a costly mistake. That's how you know God is giving you a new season. You are giving the word of God more attention.

    a. It's in your mouth

    b. You are meditating on it 24/7

    c. You are observing and doing

    – applying it to your actions

    d. You feel the presence of God (verse 9c)

Getting back into school, training for ministry, rearranging your routine, letting some things go, feeling yourself being stretched – that's all part of your new season. But the most essential factor is spiritual focus.

Verse 9 gives some guidelines for your new season: Be strong. Be courageous. Don't accept disappointment. Remember God is with you! Don't lose your focus! I have seen students come here and start a new season of their life. Then they lost their spiritual focus. Then they were defeated and dropped out...and kept on dropping. A female student from a nearby drug rehab shelter found Christ. God delivered her, and called her into the ministry. She attended here. After a while she got a work-study scholarship, and a room on campus. She became part of the inner life of the campus. Joined intercession groups, served on the praise team. Then she got gradually drawn away and lost her spiritual focus. Suddenly, she made a series of poor choices. She lost her job, dropped out, kept on dropping and went back on drugs and became a prostitute again to support her habit. That happened to Israel in the Promised Land, and it can happen to anyone here who loses that spiritual focus! Know the season and don't miss out!

WE ARE NOT CALLED FOR WHO WE ARE

"But the LORD said unto Samuel, Look not on his countenance, or on the height of his stature; because I have refused him: for the LORD seeth not as man seeth; for man looketh on the outward appearance, but the LORD looketh on the heart."
I Samuel 16:7

"Don't presume to think that you pre-qualify for what God wants to do with you!"

In this story, the prophet Samuel had been sent by the Lord to Bethehem to the family of Jesse. He knew he was to anoint one of Jesse's sons to be the next king of Israel. But he didn't know which one. As he began to meet them, he first thought it was Eliab, but the Lord said no – because, He said, don't go by his looks, or his height. "For the Lord seeth not as man seeth; for man looketh on the outward appearance, but the Lord looketh on the heart."

Then he passed over Abinadab, Shammah and seven more sons. There was one more, the very youngest, but he was out tending the sheep. This was David. Samuel asked to see him. When David came in, the Lord spoke to Samuel, "Arise anoint him, for this is he!" As Samuel did so, the Spirit of the Lord came upon David from that day forward. David was the most unlikely of all Jesse's sons. He was too young. He had not yet developed any leadership qualities. Yet God chose Him – not for who he was, but for his potential. God could see his heart, and God knew He could work with David. When I was saved, I was called into the ministry of preaching the Word. But I didn't understand it. I was a convict in prison. How could I be qualified to be a preacher? I just didn't know then that "God doesn't call the qualified – He qualifies the called."

I Corinthians 1:26 – 29 explains that. Not many wise or mighty or noble men are called. And in verses 27 and 28 God's word lists 5 categories of people He does choose.

"Foolish" means *morons*. "Weak" means *sick*. "Base" means *illegitimate*. "Despised" means *rejects*. "Things which are not" means *nobodies*. That tells me that being smart, or having it all together, coming from a good family, being well-liked by the people, or having been successful at other careers – has nothing to do with it. We weren't pre-qualified for the ministry at all. Any ability we now have that brings spiritual success is by the grace of God. It's all grace!

When God chose you He took on a construction project. Someone said, "The conversion of a soul is the miracle of a moment. The manufacture of a saint is the task of a lifetime." Let me tell you four ways that God is going to work with you to qualify you: One: Solitude – teaching the presence of God. Two: Obscurity – teaching humility. Three: Monotony – building dependability. Four: Reality – teaching empathy and compassion. All of these phases were illustrated in the life of David.

You may be in the monotony stage now. You're in a place now that requires the discipline of doing the same thing every day, every week. The routine is demanding and sometimes boring. Even that can be to your benefit. Take advantage of your time here - building good habits, discipline and faithfulness. Be patient in this process. God is changing you. You were not called for who you were. You were called for who you are becoming. Let's begin to look at those about you in the body of Christ as "becomers." We are not yet what we should be, but we have already become more than we ever were before we met Christ.

WHEN YOU ARE IN THE PLACE OF A TIGHT SQUEEZE

"David therefore departed thence, and escaped to the cave Adullam: and when his brethren and all his father's house heard it, they went down thither to him." I Samuel 22:1

"God sometimes puts us into tight places so that we can leave our past and embrace our future.

In this story David was a fugitive. In verse 10 of the preceding chapter, David fled for fear of Saul and went to Achish the king of Gath. Then at Gath, he realized he was in danger there too. So in Chapter 22:1 we see the word "therefore." Because he couldn't stay in either place, David fled into the wilderness of Judea near the Dead Sea. There he hid himself in the cave called Adullam. The name Adullam meant "place of a tight squeeze." Probably there was some passage deep inside that cave that was very narrow. I remember a time I found myself in such a tight squeeze in a cave under Grandfather Mountain in Tennessee. I was very weary with jet lag – just returning from a trip to Israel. My wife Jackie met me at the airport with a change of clothes, and drove me straight to our private Christian school, Our Shepherd's Academy. A group that included my son Doug had planned an overnight field trip to go spelunking. I really just wanted to go home and go to bed, but I had promised my son and the other students that I would go with them, and the bus was waiting for me. When we entered the cave that night the kids were full of energy and excitement. They stopped only long enough to put down their bedrolls. Away we went with some flashlights and a map of the cave. In the narrow places we had to go single file. Two chaperones went ahead and I brought up the rear.

Then it happened. They squeezed through a place called "Fat Man's Squeeze." I was too big. I was first on my hands and knees and eventually inching forward flat on my belly. Then I couldn't go forward and I couldn't back up. I knew I was stuck. The lights and voices ahead grew fainter and fainter. I had my pride. I was not about to let them know I was stuck in "Fat Man's Squeeze." In that smothering darkness, I made the Lord some promises. (One of which was to lose some weight). And he heard me and got me through! That experience was good for me. In several ways, it was a defining moment. This experience of David was a defining moment for him. Here it was that God began to send him help. He was making the sacrifice of leaving a house and possessions and family behind. Others following his example began to join him. God sent the prophet Gad and God spoke to David with new directions. God sometimes sends you through a tight squeeze to get you to leave your past and embrace your future.

Are you in a tight place right now? Look upon it as a defining moment in your life – a watershed divide in your life. In this place you cannot back up. Your life will never return to the way it was, no matter how badly you wish for it! And you can go forward only if God helps you! You simply cannot get yourself out of this difficulty by self effort. In this tight squeeze you are going to lose a lot of weight – I mean that excess baggage of stuff in your life that complicates everything. God is going to help you live more simply. And in this tight squeeze you can only go in one direction. That is toward where God wants you. In this tight squeeze, you might have to let the crowd go on without you; you might have to leave them behind; or you might have to let them go in another direction entirely. You are going to go through this alone – just you and God. And you will go in the direction He wills, at the pace He brings you. As you do you will be called upon to make some decisions and some promises. But in so doing you will be leaving your past and embracing your future.

YOU MAY HAVE TO ENCOURAGE YOUR OWN SELF

"And David was greatly distressed; for the people spake of stoning him, because the soul of all the people was grieved, every man for his sons and for his daughters: but David encouraged himself in the LORD his God." I Samuel 30:6

"There are times when your best friends, your pastor, or even the one you married cannot look up from their own struggles to notice that you need some encouragement."

David was a fugitive, chased by King Saul's army patrols.

While he hid out in the Judean wilderness near the Dead Sea, supporters began to join him. In I Samuel 22 we see that first came kinfolk. Then the "3-D" crowd came: those in distress, those in debt and those that were discontented. About 400 of these so-called "encouragers" came. Then David had to cross the border and pretend to be a guerilla fighter on the side of the Philistines. His little army grew to about 600 of the distressed, debt-ridden, and discontented. David and his men even had a village given to them by King Achish where their wives and children could come live with them. This village base camp was called Ziklag.

One day they came home and the village was in ashes. Their families gone. Suddenly these encouragers turned on David. They were getting ready to stone David for leading them into this disaster. David was already greatly distressed himself. He was grieving for his own family. But now not only is there no one encouraging him, but they all want to kill him. Verse 6 ends with a very important idea. "...But David encouraged himself in the Lord his God." And when he did things began to happen. God promised him that he would "without fail recover all" – a phrase repeated in verses 9, 18 and 19. And he did. He rescued his family, and the families of his men. Not only that, but they got all the spoil that the enemy had collected in raids on other villages. They came back with more than they lost.

"They went to the enemy's camp, and took back what the Devil stole from them!" Now, what turned that situation around? It was when David encouraged himself in the Lord his God. Some lessons here: First, you need to already have a relationship with God. Note the phrase "his God." Secondly, there are times that you may have to encourage your own self. Thirdly, when you do, it will turn the situation around. *Not just one situation.* It can turn your whole life around! Within a week of standing in the ashes of Ziklag, Saul had been killed, and David was sitting on the throne of Judah in Hebron!

Are you standing in the midst of a ruined comfort zone? Have all your encouragers failed you? Well, this is a great time for you to become an encourager. Of yourself! Do it like David did it. In Psalm 18 where the heading reads, "A psalm of David, the servant of the Lord, who spake unto the Lord the words of this song in the day that the Lord delivered him from the hand of all his enemies, and from the hand of Saul…" we find what David said in Ziklag.

"I will love thee, O Lord my strength. The Lord is my rock, and my fortress, and my deliverer; my God, my strength, in whom I will trust; my buckler, and the horn of my salvation, and my high tower. I will call upon the Lord, who is worthy to be praised…" (Ps. 18:1-3). Then in verse 6: "In my distress I called upon the Lord…." Is that what you do when you are in distress? This is a great life lesson. It requires practice to make it stick! Get started today.

THE POWER OF HENENI

"Also I heard the voice of the Lord, saying, Whom shall I send, and who will go for us? Then said I, Here am I; send me." Isaiah 6:8

"When you say to God in sincerity, 'Here I Am,' your life will tap into the greatest power of the universe. This is a statement of availability and willingness that validates your salvation and implements the Lordship principle."

In this passage we are allowed to overhear a personal conversation with God. God calls and a man wholeheartedly answers, "Heneni." This is the Hebrew phrase for "Here I am." Isaiah is only one of several in the Bible who responded to God's call with this simple phrase. Jacob said it when he was about to go into Egypt (Gen. 46:2). Moses said it at the burning bush (Ex. 3:4). Samuel said it as a child in the Tabernacle (I Sa. 3:8). We know what God did with these men when they said "Heneni." Do you know what God can do with you – if you fully and completely make yourself available?

That is hard to even imagine. We are so busy working on our own plans. God is saying who do we have that we can send? Who can we put in that gap? Who can we raise up to lead in that situation? But we scarcely pay attention – thinking surely some great Christian will step forward. "Heneni" – here I am - sets two great principles at work in your life. First: it validates your salvation. Just as faith without works is dead, faith with works is proof. If you say you are *saved through faith – you can demonstrate that by living a life of service* to God. *You once demonstrated that you were not saved* by living your life serving the Devil. Second: it implements the Lordship principle. We like to sing and say that "Jesus is Lord." Is He really?

I mean is He Lord of your life? Then if He is Lord, He is free to take you and send you anywhere. If He is Lord, he can change your career plans and retrain and redirect you. If He is Lord, your life and all you have is at His disposal.

I said "Here I Am" and God used me in planting eight US churches and over thirty Mayan churches. I said "Here I Am" and I found myself in Brazil speaking to a convention of 200,000 missionaries. I said "Here I am" and was interviewed on CBN's 700 Club twice. I said "Here I Am" and wound up preaching in the rain in Nakuru, Kenya and having breakfast with President Moi. I said "Here I Am" and preached a crusade in Haiti standing 4 hours at a time in the heat and stench with 25,000 souls crowed around me chanting "Jesu! – Jesu! –Jesu!" I said "Here I Am" and have twice given my testimony on Voice of Hope's world-wide radio broadcast to over 100 nations. I said "Here I Am" and the Lord brought me here to this college.

When the call comes from One who is absolute Lord, there is only one acceptable response. Your only proper response to the Lordship of Jesus is simply to say, "Heneni" – here I am! So this is my challenge to you today. Has it been a long time since you told Jesus you were available for anything and everything? Or have you ever said that to the Lord? Another question: has it been a while since you said, "If I'm on the wrong path, please change it for me?" Would you dare to say it now – from the heart?

A CERTAIN MOVEMENT
OF THE WIND

"And let it be, when thou hearest the sound of a going in the tops of the mulberry trees, that then thou shalt bestir thyself: for then shall the LORD go out before thee, to smite the host of the Philistines." 2 Samuel 5:24

"There are times when something you were waiting for finally happens, and you know God is at work on your behalf."

In this text, David sought an answer from God about when to go against the Philistines. God said wait until you hear the wind in the top of the mulberry trees. Then it was time to do battle because God was fighting on David's side. You may also recall that it was with a mighty east wind that God parted the Red Sea. Then it was time to cross that sea. The Holy Spirit came to the church in Acts 2 with the sound of a rushing mighty wind. Then it was time to move out and witness in power.

In the old days of sailing ships, it made good sense to wait until you had a favorable wind to launch out on a journey. Today, with diesel engines, ships press ahead regardless of wind direction. But even so a headwind can slow the progress and increase the cost by demanding more fuel. I have had a lot of experience with headwinds and tailwinds flying in small planes. Winds make a great difference. It is wise to pay attention to winds. This is especially true of spiritual winds. A spiritual wind got you saved. A spiritual wind blew on you and you felt the love of Christ and the power of his word. A spiritual wind brought you here. The moving of the Holy Spirit is always strong - moving you along with it, and blowing things out of your way!

One clear crisp day of early autumn, I stood in my backyard on our farm with my brother in law. We noticed a hawk high above, moving swiftly from one tree line to the other. As it passed over us we saw that its wings were outstretched but motionless. We commented about how still the air was down where we were, yet up where that hawk was, there was a strong movement of wind. I want to be like that hawk – discovering certain movements of God's Spirit, and riding them with no effort of my own. Just being in the right place at the right time for the right thing in God's plan.

There are spiritual wind currents in your life right now that can carry you where your own strength would fail to carry you. You just have to discover those currents. You will not find them if you are too busy to pray, read your Bible or just savor the goodness of God. Those certain movements of the wind are not for the unspiritual. But spiritual men and women can discern the movement of God's Spirit. The secret to success in any ministry is just to find out what God is doing, and do it with Him! Stop today and find out in which part of your life you can discern that certain movement of the wind. Focus on that area and maximize your efforts. You will be amazed at what God can do with you!

FALLING DOWN
AND GETTING UP

"And it came to pass in an eveningtide, that David arose from off his bed, and walked upon the roof of the king's house: and from the roof he saw a woman washing herself; and the woman was very beautiful to look upon. ...And the woman conceived, and sent and told David, and said, I am with child. ...And Nathan said to David, Thou art the man. Thus saith the LORD God of Israel, I anointed thee king over Israel, and I delivered thee out of the hand of Saul; ...And David said unto Nathan, I have sinned against the LORD. And Nathan said unto David, the LORD also hath put away thy sin; thou shalt not die. ...Then David arose from the earth, and washed, and anointed himself, and changed his apparel, and came into the house of the LORD, and worshipped: then he came to his own house; and when he required, they set bread before him, and he did eat." 2 Samuel 11:2, 5; 12:7, 9, 13, 20

"Sins of Christians have terrible consequences. Even those in ministry can fall. Some don't know how to get back up, and the consequences keep on multiplying. But David is an example of one who got back up."

In this story we can clearly see three steps into sin. First, David accidentally saw Bathsheba taking a bath. At this point he could have turned his eyes away and there would have been no sin. Second, he began to entertain lust. He asked questions about her. Third, he used his power as king and took her and used her. We can also see how quickly one sin leads to another. She conceived and told David. He arranged a military furlough for her husband Uriah, thinking he would sleep with her and no one would ever know he was not the father. Then, when that did not work, David had her husband Uriah killed and he married her.

We can also see very clearly three steps out of the sin cycle. Nathan the prophet brought David the word of God. First, David "heard" the word, which means he received it. Then, secondly, he said, "I have sinned." That's confession. Thirdly, he accepted the consequences. He was told the child would die. Other consequences would follow in later years with his children following his example. Now we can see three clear steps for getting back up and being restored. First, David prayed a sincere prayer for forgiveness, recorded in Psalm 51. Then secondly, he received God's approval. We see that in 2 Samuel 12:20. He got up, changed his apparel – a metaphor for taking the garment of joy for the spirit of heaviness - and went and worshipped God. Thirdly, he received restoration. He comforted his wife, and they conceived again. This time God blessed them and gave them Solomon.

So you can fall down, and you can get back up. David became the spiritual leader of his people and wrote psalms that we still use in worship. There may be some here who are struggling with consequences from previous sin. God will help you build a bridge over them and bless and prosper you again. The consequences of what you have already done will not go away, but you can get out of that cycle that causes them to multiply. And you can accept God's forgiveness and restoration. Jesus died on the cross for all your sin: past, present, and future. As he suffered there, his arms were outstretched as if to say, "I love you this much." The ultimate cost of your sin was the crucifixion of our Lord. But the ultimate result of the cross is your total forgiveness. Today, you can have a new beginning. A new sense of cleansing and release.

HANDFULS ON PURPOSE

"And let fall also some of the handfuls of purpose for her, and leave them, that she may glean them, and rebuke her not." Ruth 2:16

"A generous spirit that goes beyond what is expected is what makes you wealthy."

God is looking for people to bless. He especially blesses those who have a big heart. Boaz is an example of one with a big heart. In Ruth 2:1 we find that he was a mighty man of wealth. But he was not wealthy because of stinginess. He had a giving nature. And he gave more than was expected. The Scriptures in Leviticus 19:9 and 23:22 show what was expected. He was obligated to leave the grain unharvested in the corners of his field and not to go back and glean where he had already harvested. This was reserved for the poor by law. It was like a welfare tax. But Boaz could decide which poor were allowed to glean in his field.

He had his regulars, but Boaz visits the field and sees a new one. He is told she is a Moabite, new in his country. He tells her not to try to go to the fields of others. She is welcome to continue to glean in this field. She can drink out of the water jars of his laborers. She can eat lunch with them. He also gave her two very special privileges. She could even glean among the sheaves – that is – where they were still working. This was normally off limits. He even had the workers drop some handfuls on purpose for her.

That is the model God likes: handfuls on purpose. Jesus said it this way: "Give to others, and God will give to you. Indeed, you will receive a full measure, a generous helping, poured into your hands – all that you can hold. The measure you use for others is the one that God will use for you" (Luke 6:38 TEV). That's why Boaz was wealthy. God was giving back into his life in proportion to how he was giving into other lives. If you live according to this principle, you will always be giving, and you will always have enough to meet your own needs. The secret is not to think of your needs first.

Some of us here may be struggling just to pay bills. We may be tempted to hold on to the little that we have and not share any of it. But if we know God's heart and understand his promise – we will give, even sacrificially. Certainly we will have a generous spirit about sharing whatever we have with others. Today we may see an opportunity to "give a handful on purpose." It's like having a piece of bread and breaking off a piece to share with someone who has less than you have. In fact, you should pray that you will find such an opportunity – to actively look for it. Because giving is a path to blessing. If you think back, you may realize that God had people that He used as His instruments to drop "handfuls on purpose" for you, not once, but many times. God has blessed you though others. Make sure you remain part of God's channel for blessings.

THE GRATITUDE OF A DROWNING MAN

"And I said, I cried by reason of mine affliction unto the LORD, and he heard me; out of the belly of hell cried I, and thou heardest my voice." "The waters compassed me about, even to the soul: the depth closed me round about, the weeds were wrapped about my head." Jonah 2:2, 5

"Each of us should realize that like Jonah, we have been spared for a purpose – else we would have long ago been dead."

In verse 2 Jonah tells about how he felt in the whale's belly when he began to pray. Verse 5 tells how he felt just before the whale swallowed him. He said the waters closed in on him – even to the soul. That is a terrifying moment when your lungs are filling with water and you cannot breath. The darkness in closing in over you as you sink deeper and deeper. When I was about 12 years of age, I had an experience like that. Visiting with cousins on a hot day, the other boys said they were going swimming. I didn't know how to swim but went along. Off we went to a deep borrow-pit filled with dark brown water. Years ago this borrow-pit had been an excavation site for earth to build a highway. Now it was the neighborhood swimming hole. All the boys went in except me.

An older boy pulled me in, mistakenly thinking I was just dreading the coldness of the water. I threshed wildly a moment and then slipped beneath the surface. He thought I was just pretending to drown. But as my lungs started to empty, bubbles came to the top of the water. So then he and the others began to try to save me. Meanwhile, darkness closed in around me and I lost consciousness. My next memory is of lying on the ground, coughing as the boys pushed water out of my chest. I had been under the water about 10 minutes. My name is Douglas, a Gaelic name meaning "drawn out of dark waters." When my mother chose that name, she had no idea how prophetic it would be. Years after the drowning incident, I discovered the meaning of my name and became acutely aware that God has been knowing me since before I was born. He has been sparing my life because He had a purpose for it. He spared me when I was 12, and He spared me at least a half dozen other times when I should have died. Part of my joy today is that I am still alive!

Have you ever thought about all those times in your own life? If you have, you will have that same grateful spirit – the gratitude of one saved from death. Surely you know by now it is not just happenstance. You are here now, in training for ministry, because God has a life purpose for you. It should be a source of joy that God loves you that much; it should be sobering to realize following God's plan for your life is serious business. You may be reading this and realize that you too have been spared for a purpose. We should all praise God for the high value He places on our lives! But our gratitude should also lead us to live out the purpose He intended.

A   REAL   FRIEND

"A man that hath friends must shew himself friendly: and there is a friend that sticketh closer than a brother." "A friend loveth at all times..." Proverbs 18:24; Proverbs 17:17a

"Friends don't just pop into your life and announce themselves. They hang with you faithfully through some trial and then you know they are real friends."

Somewhere, I read that surveys show that the average American has 1.3 friends. If the average is that low, there must be some folk who don't have any friends at all. In fact, some must be operating at a deficit – like maybe having only enemies! Maybe, if the survey had broadened the definition of "friend," the results would have been better. There are several definitions of friends these days. One definition says, "The enemy of my enemy is my friend." Others would say that a friend is someone who likes you. But I like the biblical definition. A real friend, according to the Bible, is one who loves you at all times. This friend will stick closer than a natural brother – no matter what. When you think of all the people in your life who have been through bad and good times with you and remained faithful friends, the list is usually small.

Jamie Buckingham, who wrote the introduction to one of my books, used to explain to his church that within the church he and his wife had an inner circle of friends. He said he was not ashamed of that fact. These people had stuck by him over the years when he was wrong, supported him when he was sick, comforted him when he was hurt. They had remained friends when he and his wife separated. They helped get Jamie and Jackie back together. They had remained friends when he made administrative mistakes in the church. Their friendship allowed them to tell him when he was wrong. They would be his friends whether he was their pastor or not. He said he owed them more than he owed the average church member. He was right.

Over the years, I have had many say to me that they were my friends. But again and again I have discovered that they were fair-weather friends only. They dropped me like a hot potato if they heard a negative rumor. They moved on quickly to friendship with another person if they found that person more interesting. In the heat of a church conflict, their friendship quickly melted away. Yet during those same times, I discovered some who were true friends. When I was sick, they sat with my wife to await outcomes of tests or operations. They visited not once but several times, and called often. They took time out of their schedules to run errands for me. These were also the ones who would come by to offer counsel if they thought I was making a wrong decision. These are the ones who could be counted on, year in and year out. These are the ones that I call my friends.

But there is a Friend who sticks closer than a brother. He has promised to be with us in trouble and deliver us. He said he would never leave us nor forsake us. He promised to be with us always. Recently, I was reminded of those precious promises. I was in the hospital and going through a rough time one day. A surgical procedure had been done the night before, and a second one was done that day. I was in great pain, lying on a gurney waiting to be taken back to my room. Suddenly I became aware of a hand on my right shoulder. It was a strong hand, and brought warmth to my shoulder in that cold corridor. I thought I was alone, and was happy to know someone was there with me, just out of eyesight. I was grateful for the touch of reassurance and reached up with my left hand to touch the hand that was on my shoulder. There was no one there! That experience was repeated again later that day in my room. I am persuaded that the Lord or an angel sent by Him came to minister to me. What a Friend we have in Jesus!

If you are a Christian, you may not have many close friends, but you do have some. Treasure them; thank God for them. They are precious gifts. Never take them for granted. You should even go out of your way from time to time to just let them know you really do appreciate them. But you have one Friend greater than all the rest. He will outlast all the rest, at least in this life. He will be with you when others cannot.

He can help you in ways others would fail. Have you told Him lately how much you appreciate Him?

YOUR SPECIAL "THERE" PLACE

"And it shall be, that thou shalt drink of the brook; and I have commanded the ravens to feed thee there. ...And it came to pass after a while that the brook dried up, because there had been no rain in the land. And the word of the LORD came unto him, saying, Arise, get thee to Zarephath, which belongeth to Zidon, and dwell there: behold, I have command-ed a widow woman there to sustain thee." I Kings 17:4, 7- 9

"At any given time in your life, there is just one best place to be. That is the address to which God's blessings will be shipped. Choose any other place, and you will miss them."

It was the beginning of a severe famine. Elijah had to find a place to hide, because the wicked king Ahab was looking for him. A natural choice would have been by some cool moun-tain stream on Mt. Hermon. But God told Elijah that he had made supernatural arrangements for him at the brook Cherith. He had already commanded ravens to bring him food *there*. Ravens are voracious. They immediately choke down any food they find. But these ravens actually brought bread from someone's table to Elijah. They brought bread and meat twice every day. Elijah would have never seen those daily miracles had he chosen to go to Mt. Hermon.

When the brook dried up about 6 months later, it was a signal to move on – but where? Again God gave him specific instructions. Go to Zarephath in Sidon. God told Elijah he had already commanded a widow *there* to feed him. Well, Elijah may not have wished to go into such a pagan country as Phoenicia. But he wisely went where God told him to go. When he gets there the widow is gathering firewood for her last meal. The famine has reached this country too. But God begins to multiply the oil and meal, and continues to do so for three years. This is now definitely the "there" place for Elijah – not the brook. Had he stayed where he was, there would have been no more deliveries by the ravens, and there would be no water. Had he gone anyplace elsewhere, the daily miracles would not have happened. He had to be where God sent him.

There are some great lessons here. First, you need to know where God wants you and when he wants you to move. That means you need to develop an ability to hear from God. You need to know where is your "there" place. That is your place of position. Second, your "there" place becomes the only place of provision. Third, it is also the only place for your preparation for the later phases of your life. The daily miracles of provision and the reviving of the dead son prepared Elijah for his awesome Mt. Carmel ministry.

For the time being, this is your "there" place. God sent you here. You are in position. So it is while you are here that God will make provision for you. And you are now being prepared for something greater in your life. You have found your special "there" place. You should have a release from worry and fear. Your blessings are being shipped to the right address! It would be good to just stop now and thank God for His place of position, provision, and preparation!

SPIRITUAL DEPRESSION AND RECOVERY

"But he himself went a day's journey into the wilderness, and came and sat down under a juniper tree: and he requested for himself that he might die; and said, It is enough; now, O LORD, take away my life; for I am not better than my fathers." I Kings 19:4

"When you think it's the end – it can be just a new beginning."

There are times when you just cannot go on. You no longer have any vision for ministry. There is no passion that drives you. That's spiritual depression. It results from not embracing a new assignment. But God will intervene and start you on the new assignment and a new path. Elijah was depressed. For the last three and a half years he had lived in preparation for a confrontation with King Ahab and the prophets of Baal who had taken over the kingdom. That was his only focus. Now it was over. The confrontation on Mt. Carmel was now history. He had successfully challenged Baalism and had called down fire from heaven in an awesome display of God's power. The prophets of Baal had been destroyed. But now he was running for his life from Queen Jezebel.

He felt like his life mission was over. The peak of his ministry was already past. It was enough. He just wanted to die. But God was not through with him. He did not know it, but his greatest ministry still lay ahead. There are some great lessons here. Elijah was exhausted. God sent an angel, not once, but twice to refresh him. Strengthened by angel food, he walked the next forty days until he got to Mt. Sinai in the Horeb range. He found a cave. He was going to live there. He knew God had been on this mountain with Moses. He wanted an experience like Moses had: God speaking like a great trumpet, the mountain on fire and the earth shaking. God spoke to him, asked him, "What are you doing here, Elijah?" - and told him to get out of the cave. Then came the great wind, then the great earthquake, then the fire. But God was not in any of that. Finally he heard a still small voice. It said the same thing: "What are you doing here, Elijah?"

Then the depressed prophet proceeds to explain to God how bad the situation was back in Israel. And all God's prophets had been killed – Elijah was his very last one. But God just told him to go back and go past Israel to Damascus. There he was to anoint the next king of Syria. Then he was to anoint the next king of Israel. Then he was to anoint the next prophet, Elisha. Then God informed Elijah that he was not the only one left. He still had 7,000 faithful servants in Israel. Here we can learn some great lessons. Lesson one: you don't have the whole picture. God does. Lesson two: you are not as ready to die as you might think you are. There's a lot more to be done. Lesson three: God won't hold a discussion with you in the cave of depression. You have to come out of the hole to hear what He has for you. Lesson four: you may not ever die. You could get raptured. Lesson five: God gives you the desires of your heart: Elijah wanted a Moses experience. Well, 950 years later, he did. He was on a mountaintop in Galilee with Moses and Jesus!

Have you reached a point in your life where you have lost your joy? Has your passion for serving Christ waned? Could it be *you* are like this prophet? Are you depressed and feel like your best days are over? Do you have no exciting vision for your future that occupies your thoughts and dreams? Are you in a spiritual hole? Then someone should say to you, "What are you doing here? Get back to that for which God has called you. God has much more to do with your life. After all that Jesus did for you, how could you even think about giving up now?"

SOME SALT WOULD MAKE IT BETTER!

"And he said, Bring me a new cruse, and put salt therein. And they brought it to him. And he went forth unto the spring of the waters, and cast the salt in there, and said, Thus saith the LORD, I have healed these waters; there shall not be from thence any more death or barren land." 2 Kings 2:20-21

"Salt is a symbol of the Holy Spirit. We have all seen some min-istries that could use a lot more salt! Is there any barrenness in your life? Some salt would make it better."

Elisha was just doing what God told him to do. And God was giving us an object lesson on the Holy Spirit. There's a lot of symbolism here. The spring is our heart. Jesus said, "As a man thinketh in his heart, so is he." "Out of the abundance of the heart the mouth speaketh." So what happens when your words and activities have no salt? They produce only barren-ness and death.

The salt is the Holy Spirit. In Ezra 7:22, there is an interest-ing item in Ezra's bill of lading for supplies authorized by the King of Persia. He could take out of the King's warehouse and carry back to Judah all those items that were specified by number or weight. But he could have "salt without prescrib-ing how much." How much of the Holy Spirit do you need? That's the idea. Jesus also used this figure of salt as a symbol of the Holy Spirit. What Jesus said in Mark 9:49-50 makes no sense if you do not know that He's talking about the Holy Spirit. He says every one shall be salted with fire – another symbol of the Holy Spirit. Then he says every sacrifice has to be sacrificed with salt – a reference to what made the Levitical sacrifices acceptable to God. Then he says we are to have salt in ourselves – and that's connected with having peace with one another.

The Scripture says in Col. 4:6 that even our speech is to be seasoned with salt. You should let the Holy Spirit make a difference in what you say to others. Not just your sermons, but your conversations. You should be giving words of wisdom, words of knowledge, prophetic encouragement! My ministry began to be real and effective only after the filling of the Holy Spirit. Before, I could get people to start, but I couldn't help them continue. I could build church membership, but I couldn't build people. One night on a plane, I sought a greater blessing, and God put some salt in me. I started truly loving people. I started having real faith. I stopped getting up sermons for Sunday, and just started taking down messages. God started working miracles through me. My fruit began to remain.

It may be that someone here has been doing everything the hard way. And it isn't working. And you are so frustrated you could quit. Some salt would make it better. Jesus loves you. He is the answer to everything. He is the Baptizer in the Spirit. With the same faith with which you took him as Saviour, you can take him as the giver of the Holy Spirit. The sooner the better. There's too much barrenness and death. Some spiritual salt will make your ministry produce life! And that's because it will release new life in you! Why not pray for Jesus to come and do for your heart what Elisha did for the fountain? Why not do it now?

MAKE YOUR VALLEY FULL OF DITCHES

"And he said, Thus saith the LORD, Make this valley full of

ditches. For thus saith the LORD, Ye shall not see wind, neither shall ye see rain; yet that valley shall be filled with water, that ye may drink, both ye, and your cattle, and your beasts." 2 Kings 3:16-17

"Just ahead of every flash flood of God's blessings, there is a period of expectation and hard work. Certain blessings cannot be received if there is no preparation for them."

Mesha the king of Moab had angered Jehoram, king of Israel. So Jehoram got the kings of Judah and Edom to help him lead a joint military expedition against Moab. But they got into trouble just before they got to the kingdom of Moab. They found themselves without water in a dry valley. They sought the Lord through the prophet Elisha. The Lord said, "Make this valley full of ditches." He was going to send water, but it would be in the form of a flash flood. It was already raining somewhere up in the mountains, although where they were the sky was clear. The flood would come suddenly and without warning. Of course the flood would quickly pass through the level valley floor – leaving no pools behind. If they expected to get any of that water, they were going to have to dig some ditches as reservoirs. That is the way some opportunities of blessing from the Lord will come. When a flood of God's blessing comes, it comes all at once! Are you going through a dry place right now? Let me ask you, have you been digging any ditches lately?

Some pastors want a hundred people to join their church

this Sunday. But they haven't trained any workers to deal with that many new members. They haven't even got that much extra parking space. They don't have the right size nursery. They don't even have enough restroom facilities. Without any of the necessary preparation, a sudden surge in membership would be like a flash flood. It would quickly run off, since there is no way to receive it. Some students want a large ministry. It's even been prophesied over them. But they haven't dug any ditches! They still don't have the right training. They concentrate on a degree instead of training. They haven't done any really hard work. For those who can receive this, let me just say that for some students doing a course paper right can be like digging ditches. But they don't see how doing this research and putting these ideas together is preparation for teaching or preaching, so they try to avoid it or just scrape by with a low grade.

Many believers are praying for more of God in their life. Yet they also want to hold on to everything the way it is. That won't work. Some things in your life have to be dug out to make room for the blessings you want. Perhaps you just haven't thought it through. But surely when you think about it, you'll realize that the more you empty your life of trivial and worldly things, the more time and space you will have for spiritual things. If you genuinely thirst for a flash flood of God's blessings, this passage gives you some important principles to follow. Here they are. One: If you're in a dry place you will learn to seek help from the Lord. Two: Even if your blessings have been prophesied, you still won't get them if you don't work. Three: You have to have faith to dig a ditch in a desert. Four: The digging always involves removal of something. Five: Expect the blessing even when there are no external signs that it's coming. Six: When it comes it will still be more than you expect.

How dry is your valley? Wouldn't it be wonderful if God would just send a flash flood of blessings? Let me ask you, are you willing to dig some ditches in your life to make room for them? Some students don't even make room in their weekly routine for course study. I'm thinking about students who add the load of college courses to an already busy schedule without giving anything up. They don't want to say no to anybody. They get caught up in a rat race of unplanned activities. They still want to watch television. They still want take whole evenings to attend special events. They still want to take all their trips. They are busy launching ministries they are not ready for, they are trying to create financial provision by taking side jobs or starting new businesses. If you are one of those, this word is for you. God's already got some rain falling. A flood is coming. Make some room for it. Dig some ditches! Why not pray now for God's wisdom about which things to remove from your life. Then pray for a mighty flash flood of God's awesome blessings.

WHAT'S ALREADY IN YOUR HOUSE?

"And Elisha said unto her, What shall I do for thee? Tell me, what hast thou in the house? And she said, Thine handmaid hath not any thing in the house, save a pot of oil." 2 Kings 4:2

"You already have more than you think you have. One of the names of God is El Shaddai – the God who is more than enough!"

The widow was desperately poor. But Elisha started by asking what she already had. It didn't make sense to him that the widow of a man of God was left with absolutely nothing. God lovingly cares and provides for all believers, but in His Word He has given many very precious promises to widows. Her answer was part unbelief. She said, "not *any* thing" – and then she said, "save a pot of oil." She *did* have something already in the house. And it was *all* that was needed. This situation may describe you. You have focused too much on what you don't have. You've overlooked what you do have. Little is much if God blesses it. This story reminds us about the time a crowd of hungry people surrounded Jesus and he told the disciples to feed them. They thought they didn't have anything at all. But a small boy had brought his lunch. And that, plus Jesus, was all they needed.

Many times I had people desiring to go on a mission with me. "But," they said sadly, "I don't have any money for a trip like that." First of all, when we look at the biblical models for short term missions, we find that in Matthew 10 and Luke 10 Jesus expressly told the disciples not to carry money with them. Their needs would be provided as they went along. In the first 1900 years of Christianity, Christian workers walked, rode horseback, or went by ship. Now, however, we have become spoiled and lazy. We are willing to do missions only if we can travel in the style to which we have become accustomed! What would you do if you knew God wanted you to go to Mexico and you did not have funds to fly? Would you even consider a bus ride?

Yet, for many destinations flying is the only means available to us. In that case, "where God guides, He also provides." And regarding some such missions people often see the lack of money as a barrier. They offer it to me as an excuse for not going. Sometimes God gives me a word about them. I ask them, "Don't you have a ring you no longer wear – that you could sell?" Or, "don't you have some money saved for a vacation?" Or, "What if you had a garage sale for a couple of weekends – putting some good useable household items back into circulation?" On those occasions we learn that they already have what God has provided for the trip. They have the provision – the pot of oil.

But this passage also has a spiritual application and in this case it is very obvious, since oil is a symbol of the Holy Spirit. This widow represents carnal Christians who cannot function healthily. They seemingly don't have what it takes to meet the challenges of a victorious and joyful life. Among such people, there are many seeking the Infilling, or the Baptism of the Spirit. They go to the altar every service. They go to all the meetings of great men and women of God. Still, not much happens. They feel empty and they claim to be empty. Does this sound familiar? Are we speaking about you?

Actually, if you are born again you already have the earnest of the Spirit. In fact "if any man have not the Spirit of Christ, he is none of his." That's your pot of oil. So – what do you have already in your house? What part of your life is purely of Christ? Not your nature at all? There's something already in you that has a love for the Word of God, a desire to please the Father, an eagerness to talk about Jesus your Lord! Why not let Christ multiply that Spirit into other parts of your life! Into your mind, will, and emotions. Like the widow, *you* do the pouring – not some great prophet. You don't wait for some feeling. *You* pour the Word into your mind. *You* pour yieldedness into your will through worship, and the joy of the Lord into your emotions through praise. *You* do the pouring – *He* does the multiplying – until you are full and running over! And probably in a very special moment sometime soon, you will suddenly realize that you are *full!* That's when you won't be able to contain yourself!

IS IT REALLY WELL WITH YOUR SOUL?

"Run now, I pray thee, to meet her, and say unto her, Is it well with thee? Is it well with thy husband? Is it well with the child? And she answered, It is well:" 2 Kings 4:26

"Sometimes you just have to shut something up in a room with God, close the door, and say, 'It is well with my soul.'"

That's what this mother did when her only son died. She took him to the room they had added on to their house for the man of God Elisha. She laid him on the bed and shut the door on him. She went to see Elisha. As she approached, Elisha's servant Gehazi asked her, is it well with you? Is it well with your husband? Is it well with the child? And she kept answering, "It is well." We know she felt great anguish. Elisha said that her soul was vexed. But she knew that God was in charge. No matter how this story ended, it was going to be well. She had turned the entire situation over to God. She had shut the door on the matter. It was all up to God. Whatever God did would be acceptable to her. That's why she could say, "It is well."

A thing like this is a huge faith test. Could you pass this kind of a test and say, "It is well?" How much does God know? Did He not know this was going to happen? How big is your God? He can do anything but fail. How great is his love? He would never hurt you nor withhold a good thing. According to Psalm 84:11, he will withhold no good thing. That means that right now, nothing that is good *by God's standard* is missing from your life. Now stop to consider how you feel about current problems and hardships. Is your heart in turmoil and tension? Are you feeling discouraged, defeated or depressed? Is it really well with your soul? What kind of expressions do you hear yourself saying? Are they positive or negative? Are you passing your faith test?

At times, a thing that we think is bad – is just the middle of an experience that is good for our souls. In Romans 8:28 God tells us that *all* things are working together for our good. That means hard things too. The Shunamite woman was going through something very hard, but her faith in God was unshaken. There is a song we often sing in church. The title is "It Is Well." The words were penned about 150 years ago by a wealthy industrialist named Horatio Spafford. He and his family planned a vacation in Great Britain. But since he had some business to conclude, he sent his wife and three daughters ahead on a ship. He planned to follow them the next week.

But in the middle of the Atlantic, the ship went down and his wife was one of the few survivors. The three daughters went down with the ship. After rescue, she arrived in England and wired her husband. "All lost but me. Please come quickly." He took the next ship, which was part of the same shipping line. The captain stopped the ship directly over the place where the sister ship had gone down, to have a memorial service. Spafford looked down over the rails and stared in to the churning sea where his three daughters were lost. The words came to him, *"When peace like a river attendeth my way, When sorrows like sea billows roll; Whatever my lot, Thou has taught me to say, It is well, it is well with my soul."* That's the kind of faith we need for trials and hardships in this life, and that's the kind of faith that will see us all the way home to heaven.

DON'T HINDER
GOD'S BLESSING

"But Naaman was wroth, and went away, and said, Behold, I thought, He will surely come out to me, and stand, and call on the name of the LORD his God and strike his hand over the place, and recover the leper. Are not Abana and Pharpar, rivers of Damascus, better than all the waters of Israel? May I not wash in them, and be clean? So he turned and went away in a rage." 2 Kings 5:11-12

"God is in the blessing business. But if we are not careful, we can hinder the very thing we need so much."

Naaman was the commander in chief of the armies of Syria, the dominant military power in the Middle East. He was a decorated hero. He was a brave soldier. But he was a leper. Nobody in Syria could help him. But a little maid that had been captured in Israel and brought back as a slave in Naaman's house remembered that there was a man of God in Israel named Elisha. She knew that Elisha's God could heal Naaman. Naaman was in good with his king, so he got a letter from the king of Syria. It was to the king of Israel, asking that Naaman be healed of his leprosy.

The king of Israel was afraid Syria was picking an excuse for starting another war – he tore his clothes in despair. But Elisha heard about it and sent word that he should send Naaman to him. Now picture this: the humble dwelling of the prophet. Riding up to his house early one morning in a splendid chariot with a huge procession following, Naaman parks in front of Elisha's house. Elisha sends out a messenger saying, "Just go on down to the Jordan river (miles away). Dip in it seven times and you will be healed." Naaman was furious. This Israelite holy man did not even show the respect of coming out to his chariot. He didn't quiver his hand over the place and shake and call on his God. He just wanted Naaman to go and dip seven times in the muddy Jordan river. A simple faith step. Something like that is often required before the blessing will come. But Naaman lashed his horses and drove off in a really foul mood. He knew he was not about to do such a humiliating thing. Servants helped him cool off and talked him into going ahead with it. And he got his healing. It was miraculous. But he almost missed it.

Here we see some things that can hinder us from receiving the blessing. First of all, anger will always take you in the wrong direction – away from the blessing. Second, the blessing can be hindered by having a closed mind of exactly where and when and how you are supposed to get the blessing. He thought Elisha was supposed to come out and take a dramatic stance, calling on God while quivering his hand over the leprosy. That's what he had in mind, and when it didn't happen, he was ready to leave. Third, you can hinder your blessing by having what you think is a better idea than what is proposed by God. If dipping in the muddy Jordan was so healthful, why not just go back to the clear mountain streams of Syria? But of course he would have missed his miracle entirely. Fourth, you can miss out on your blessing by being guided by whether the faith step is convenient. He had already come a long way. It was miles further on to the Jordan river.

On the positive side, he did humble himself and get the blessing. But only after he went all the way to the Jordan, and only after he dipped his whole body, and only after all seven times as Elisha instructed. We can learn a couple of useful principles here. First, there is humility – recognizing you have nothing to barter with and are just depending on the mercy of God, is absolutely necessary. Secondly, you have to completely obey. Obedience is still disobedience if it is not complete. Somebody here may be just a few steps away from getting the blessing, but you need to do all that God told you in His word to do. Check yourself through prayer and meditation: are you hindering your own blessing? Have you overlooked some areas of disobedience? Is your pride hindering your blessing? What a wonderful day this can be – if you finally receive that great blessing you could have already had!

ANOINTED TO THE BONE

"And it came to pass, as they were burying a man, that, behold, they spied a band of men; and they cast the man into the sepulcher of Elisha: and when the man was let down, and touched the bones of Elisha, he revived, and stood up on his feet." 2 Kings 13:21

"Some things should be more than skin-deep. The anointing of God is like that."

Elisha trained under Elijah. When God was calling Elijah home to heaven, Elisha just wanted one thing – a double portion of the spiritual anointing that was on Elijah. He had a desire for a good thing. He wanted the power of God in his life. And he received it. He had such a powerful presence of God's spirit that he *even had it in his bones*. And when he died and all that was left of his body was just the bones, those old bones still had the anointing. God could still use them for His glory.

The anointing of God allows you to do something good and powerful, even when you don't know you're doing it. That's because it's not you. It's God. The problem with so many believers is that they allow so little of God's anointing to get into them. For some, it's not even skin deep. It's just put-on. Others have a little in their skin – enough to make another person tingle a little. But only a few in each generation have the anointing even in their bones. When they get old and frail in the flesh, they still have the power of God in their bones! Your bones are your very foundation. Even the blood is produced in your bone marrow. When you have so much of something that it's even in your bones, you have all you can have! So we have expressions like "bad to the bone," or, "ugly to the bone." But we should have another expression: anointed to the bone!"

How does one become anointed to the bone? First of all you must desire it above any other desire. That was Elisha. He gave up his big farming operation. He killed a yoke of oxen, used the plows for firewood and made a feast to celebrate going into the ministry. There was no going back. He stuck with the great man of God Elijah and desired the anointing that was on him. You have to want to be holy unto the Lord. Secondly, you must stay in a spiritual atmosphere. With Elijah, he was constantly in ministry, but he was also sitting in the schools of prophets taught by Elijah. You have to make some choices to stay in a spiritual atmosphere. Sometimes you have to pay a price. You sacrifice the life you could have lived in the flesh.

Thirdly, you must learn to pay more attention to that spiritual atmosphere than you do your physical environment. When he was about to be carried up, Elijah told Elisha that if he could still see him when he went into the spiritual dimension, he would know he had the double anointing. And he saw the chariot of fire and horses of fire. Then when the army of Syrians surrounded his house and his servant became afraid, Elisha could say, "Fear not: for they that be with us are more than they that be with them." He could see the spiritual realities. An angelic army with horses and chariots of fire surround Elisha's house.

Is your spirituality only skin deep, or are you anointed to the bone? May you be like Jeremiah, and get the fire of God down into your very bones! There are so many trivial things pressing for your time and energy. But if you really want the anointing this is how you get it: Separating yourself, walking in obedience, desiring more of God and less of the world. Staying in the presence so long that you become saturated with it – down to the bone. Some of you students already are on your way to that kind of anointing. That's why you are here at this college. God has stirred your heart and now you can no longer be satisfied with the level of spirituality you had in the past. You, like Elisha, are asking for a greater anointing. Here is a word for you: as you develop a greater hunger for God's anointing, you will be creating the capacity for it. God is more ready than you are!

WHAT YOU GIVE GOD HAS TO COST SOMETHING

"And king David said to Ornan, Nay; but I will verily buy it for the full price: for I will not take that which is thine for the LORD, nor offer burnt offerings without cost." I Chronicles 21:24

"There's no such thing as cheap grace, and there's no such thing as cheap Christianity."

David had to buy Ornan's threshing floor. God told him to do it and set up an altar there. So he asked Ornan to sell to him for the full price. Ornan says, "Just take it – no charge." You can even have the oxen for sacrifice and the threshing flails for wood. "I give it all." Ornan had the right attitude. If it's for God, no cost is too great. But David was not about to offer God something that has cost him nothing. He paid 600 shekels of gold for it. He built an altar and offered a sacrifice which God accepted by sending fire from heaven. In 2nd

Samuel 24:24 David says, "...Neither will I offer burnt offerings unto the Lord my God of that which doth cost me nothing." It had to cost him something.

This is a Bible principle. Abraham loved God, but he needed to demonstrate that love by a sacrifice. All the pagan Canaanites around him believed that if they really loved their god, they would be willing to sacrifice their son. Did Abraham love his God as much as they loved theirs? That's the question settled by the story in Genesis 22. Interestingly, the place on Mount Moriah where Abraham came to offer Isaac, is the same spot that David bought from Ornan the Jebusite. At that place Abraham prophesied that "in this mountain of the Lord it shall be seen." And he named it Jehovah-Jireh ("the Lord will provide"). And in David's time, that's where God stopped the plague of death on the people.

Even more interesting is that this is the same mountain on which Jesus would be lifted up on a cross. And there God provided the ransom that Abraham prophesied. And there God stopped the plague of eternal death on your soul. But in all these stories, the sacrifice had to cost something. You cannot please God with an offering that costs you nothing! God gave His only Son. What have you given him? David wanted his offering to have some material cost. Of course there was a tremendous emotional cost to Abraham to be willing to offer his son. And who can understand the pain in God's heart as He saw His only Son dying on the cross?

In the first year of a church that God led me to plant, we asked for sacrificial giving so that we could purchase some property and build a house of worship. A poor widow brought the price of a warm winter coat that she had been saving for. She was willing to face the winter chill without that coat in order to give something to God. I know hundreds of stories like hers. In fact, we planted several churches, and not one could be successfully planted without sacrifice. My family sacrificed so that I could serve with little or no salary. The people saw our example and they sacrificed too. But these early fellowships were filled with love that money could not buy. And oh, how God blessed us.

Yet today when a young man enters the ministry, and gets his first interview about a church position – he right away wants to know about his financial package. He's not thinking about sacrifice. If anything, in his mind the church should sacrifice to get someone like him! I'm here today to remind you that any good thing you do for God that truly blesses and glorifies Him – will have to cost you something! Perhaps God has been speaking to your heart about something you're holding on to. But you need to make a sacrifice so that God can bless you. In your prayer time today, why not settle it in your heart that you will gladly do that thing God wants, no matter what it will cost you?

GOD IS LOOKING FOR SOMETHING

"For the eyes of the LORD run to and fro throughout the whole earth, to show himself strong in the behalf of them whose heart is perfect toward him. Herein thou hast done foolishly: therefore from henceforth thou shalt have wars." 2 Chronicles 16:9

"It's not so much about how perfect your life is right now; it is much more about the attitude of your heart. God is checking you out right now."

The Word of the Lord came through Hanani the seer to Asa, king of Judah. He had relied on the Lord in the past but now had backslidden and sought help from the king of Syria. Part of that word is in verse 9. Actually it means that the eyes of the Lord are darting rapidly back and forth, looking for people who have perfect hearts. *It indicates that he might have already looked at you hundreds of time in the last millisecond – just to see if there has been some minute change.* He wants to show himself. He wants to show himself to be mighty. He just needs one thing: a perfect heart.

Here we see God's goal in your life: He wants to reveal himself through your obedience. We know that partial obedience is still disobedience. Delayed obedience is disobedience. But now we see that half-hearted obedience is not enough either. It must be whole-hearted. It's about attitude! Are any changes taking place in your heart toward God? Have you almost changed enough that the Lord is about to show himself strong in your behalf? What would it take for you to have all your heart in God's hands? A funeral? Loss of your health or your wealth? When will you learn to depend only upon God?

I was in jail when Christ saved me. He got me out. I was homeless. He gave me shelter. I was hungry. He fed me. I have been sick. He healed me. I was a nobody. He called me into the ministry. At times I was called to plant a church with no certain income. I always said, "pay the bills and the missions support first." Sometimes there was nothing left for me, my wife and two small children. But God took care of us. We raised two children with out a health care policy. We ate whatever was left on the doorstep by church members.

I have lost my health and gone through years of suffering with Lupus. When I was dying in a hospital, God healed me. After that, I had fifteen years of perfect health: without even a sore throat. About a year and a half ago, they took CT scans and found tumors. They took a needle biopsy. They did exploratory surgery. Found no cancer. Recently, I had a heart attack. It went undiagnosed for 11 days and part of my heart muscle was damaged more because of the delay. There was no way to repair it. They put some stints in on the other side of my heart and increased the blood flow there, but about one third of my heart was atrophied. But God has brought me back again. I have been in many situations where God was the only one who could help me. And then, and then – he showed himself strong in my behalf! God is looking at you right now. What does he see? Let Him see a heart that is fully focused on Him as your only hope.

WHEN YOU DON'T KNOW
WHAT TO DO

"O our God, wilt thou not judge them? For we have no might against this great company that cometh against us; neither know we what to do; but our eyes are upon thee." 2 Chronicles 20:12

"There have been times when you were in trouble and you didn't know how to fix it. You tried and you only made it worse. But God had the answer."

Think back on those times as we look at this passage. Here we can see seven steps to victory when you don't know what to do. Step one is in verse 13. Open your mind to the prophetic or *rhema* word of God. Here the people gathered before the Lord, and the Spirit of the Lord came upon Jahaziel and God gave a word through him. What a great encouragement that word was! That's step one: Openness to the Word. The answer to what to do is given in a word from God. Today we can still get it the way it happened here. But we can also get it on our knees alone – just listening in the Spirit. Especially when we have our Bibles open.

Step two is in verses 17 and 20. Specific instructions are received, and specific obedience follows. Just do what God says to do. So step two is Obedience. Right here is where you can lose it. You already know you don't know what to do. But still you will question a clear word from God – even when it is confirmed through more than one source. If Judah had not fully obeyed these odd but effective instructions, their nation would have been overrun by the enemy.

Step three follows in verses 21 and 22. Honor God with public praise. They sent out praisers ahead of the fighting men. They praised the Lord; they praised him for his mercy; and they praised the beauty of holiness. And that alone drove the enemy into confusion. Step three, then, is Oral Praise. Can you go right in front of the enemy and talk about how great and good God is? If you can, there's a chance God is about to give you an awesome victory!

Then step four follows in verse 24. They just observed what God did. They got up in a watchtower and looked, and saw what God had done. They enemy was destroyed. God had fought their battle for them. The fourth step is Observation. They had the victory – just handed to them by the Lord. Dr. Chand often says, "If you see a turtle on a fence post, you know he didn't get there by himself!" But sometimes we forget God and think we got some great idea or did some great thing. It is extremely necessary to observe and remember what God has done.

Now the fifth step is in verse 25. They gathered the precious jewels and other riches that were found on the slain army. It took them three days, and they had more than they could carry. This is the step of Obtaining. They gained from the experience. They got something out of all the trouble. God intends for you to always profit from an attack of the enemy by not only overcoming, but also obtaining either new territory, or new financial strength, or new wisdom.

The sixth step is in verse 26. On the day after they finished gathering the spoils of victory, they gathered in the valley of Berachah and blessed the Lord. This is the step of Obligation. Raised in the southern US in a period very different from today, I learned very early the custom of saying, "Much obliged" whenever being extended a kindness. It meant that you were indebted to someone for their help, and at the very least you must acknowledge the fact by saying, "Much obliged." You said it if someone gave you a lift in their car. You said it if they only opened a door for you. Of course God had done far more than that for Judah. Now they were obliged to thank the Lord and bless his Holy Name for what He had done. Speaking to God directly and just thanking him is not only a proper obligation – it's just plain courtesy!

The seventh step is found in the next verse (27): Open Joy. Their triumphal procession through Jerusalem to the Temple was joyful and it was open. How long has it been since you took your joy in the Lord outside? Have people ever seen you really happy and excited about something God did in your life? That's how we should be witnessing. I think we should so conduct ourselves every day that those around us see a consistent attitude of gratitude. Our openness in praising God should become infectious. Others ought to be drawn into the spirit of thankfulness by our example.

This was a victory so complete that it resulted in the fear of God in all the neighboring kingdoms and it brought peaceful quiet and rest to the reign of Jeshoshaphat. When God does something, he does it completely. If we win a battle, we will have to face another one with the same enemy again and again. But when God steps in, he settles things! I want to praise God for all the victories he has won for me in my life! I praise him for the things he has forever settled for me! Don't you feel that way too?

WHEN A NATION PRAYS

"If my people, which are called by my name, shall humble themselves, and pray, and seek my face, and turn from their wicked ways; then will I hear from heaven, and will forgive their sin, and will heal their land." "Then there came some that told Jehoshaphat, saying, There cometh a great multitude against thee from beyond the sea on this side Syria; and behold, they be in Hazazontamar, which is Engedi. And Jehoshaphat feared, and set himself to seek the LORD, and proclaimed a fast throughout all Judah. And Judah gathered themselves together, to ask help of the LORD: even out of all the cities of Judah they came to seek the LORD. And Jehoshaphat stood in the congregation of Judah and Jerusalem, in the house of the LORD, before the new court, And said, O LORD God of our fathers, art not thou God in heaven? And rulest not thou over all the kingdoms of the heathen? And in thine hand is there not power and might, so that none is able to withstand thee?" 2 Chronicles 7:14; 20: 3-6

"There are positive turning points in the history of a nation that

only God can arrange, and he will only do it if the believers of that country gather in concerted repentance and prayer. I personally witnessed such a turning point in our own nation, and it showed me the power of national prayer."

Here is an example in scripture of national humility and prayer in a time of national crisis. In II Chronicles 20, it was the crisis hour for the nation of Judah. Jehoshaphat the king led the nation in a call to fasting and prayer. Then in front of the entire national assembly, he himself led in a heartfelt prayer to God. He was trusting in the promise of God made back in 2 Chronicles 7:14. In the resulting story, God miraculously delivered Judah from the joint invasion of Moab and Ammon. Had Jehoshaphat not led the nation to pray, Judah would have been destroyed at that time.

I remember our national crisis of 1980, in the last year of Jimmy Carter's presidency. The oil-hungry Soviet Union had invaded Afghanistan in a desperate gamble to gain a foothold in the rich oil fields of the Persian Gulf. Carter threatened war with the Soviets if they made any further movement into the Gulf area. He cancelled the Olympics that were scheduled for Moscow. He limited the sale of grain to the Soviet Union. He ordered new nuclear weapons to be installed in Western Europe. The entire world seemed on the threshold of nuclear war. Islamic fundamentalists overthew the Shah of Iran. The Ayatollah Khomeini took over. Militant Iranians stormed the American Embassy in Teheran and took 50 Americans captive. In April, special forces tried to rescue them. It was a disastrous failure and the mission had to be aborted: eight Americans died in the fiery crash of a transport plane and a helicopter in the Iranian desert.

Oil exports from Iran stopped. The cost of imported oil to the US doubled. As a result, the economy of America was suffering from sharply rising inflation. Interest rates rose. Unemployment went over 7 percent for the nation and 13 per cent for Black Americans. It was an election year and our nation was severely divided. Leaders from the Christian Broadcasting Network, Trinity Broadcasting Network, PTL Network, Full Gospel Businessmen's Fellowship and leadership from several large denominations proclaimed a day of prayer on Monument Mall in Washington. My daughter Teresa and I were present among the one million people who gathered that day to pray.

It was an awesome sight. A million souls – all representing large groups back home who could not afford the journey – repented and prayed. They repented that we had allowed the slaughter of babies by abortion to go unchallenged, that we had allowed homosexuality to be honored in our society, that we had not depended upon God in our national and foreign policies. They prayed that God would have mercy and spare our nation, release the hostages. But unlike the story in the Bible, our national leader did not participate in the national day of prayer – even though he was only a few blocks away at the time. Simply because he was the president and also because he was an avowed religious man, Carter was invited to come and help lead in prayer. Everyone thought he would surely come. It was explained to us that he was too busy, try-ing to free the hostages.

God answered the prayer, but Carter lost the election. Reagan won by a landslide and the hostages were immediate-ly released. Inflation dropped. Russians were turned back in Afghanistan. The Soviet leader Breshnev died. The tensions with the Soviets relaxed. Soon the Berlin wall would be torn down. Soon the Soviet empire would collapse. America would become strong again. God had turned it around! What happens to nations is also what happens to individuals. If you are going through a dark time, your one best hope is not to work so hard on trying to turn it around with your own wis-dom and effort, but to simply stop and make yourself fully accountable to God. Repent of every known sin. Pray for mercy. Ask God to turn it around. He said He would. Do you believe Him?

CUT A PATH AND LEAVE A TRAIL

"And he did that which was right in the sight of the LORD, according to all that his father Amaziah did. And he sought God in the days of Zechariah, who had understanding in the visions of God: and as long as he sought the LORD, God made him to prosper." 2 Chronicles 26: 4, 5

"If you're doing right and people around you aren't, you have to cut a new path and blaze a trail for others to follow."

The previous king of Judah, Amaziah, had become an idolater and brought the whole country down. Uzziah, at age 16, was made to be king. He had a spiritual advisor named Zechariah. Though he was young, he did what was right. But the royal court was loaded with those who had supported Amaziah and his idolatrous ways. Society around him had gotten accustomed to living as heathen. Most of the people in Uzziah's life as he began his reign probably resisted him for doing what was right.

Nevertheless, he succeeded in turning the whole country around, and had a successful reign for 52 years. At the end of his reign, he made a big mistake by getting out of his calling and doing what only a priest should do. He was stricken with leprosy and died in disgrace. But for 52 years he had great success. That is outstandingly remarkable when compared to reigns of other kings of his time. Now, the word *prosper* at the end of verse five is from a very interesting Hebrew word – one which means "to push forward and break out." He broke out of the mold of his father and the society of his time. What did this young king have going for him, so that he overcame the moral and spiritual decadence of his time and prospered while doing the right thing? We can see it all in verse 5. There we see three things: the power of a godly passion, the influence of a godly friend, and the condition of God's blessing.

If you're going to make a difference with your life, you will need all three. First there is the godly passion. Uzziah *sought* God. That word in verse 5 comes from a Hebrew word which means to cut a path and leave a trail. When I was traveling with a group through dense jungle in the Yucatan, we had a small team of Maya men with machetes moving ahead of us in the right direction, cutting a trail for the rest of us to follow. It was hard going for them, but their hard work made it easy for us to follow. That's what the word *sought* means here. Uzziah had a passion to know the will of God, and he pursued it.

That brings us to the second thing: influence of a godly friend. There was an older man of God, Zechariah, who had understanding in the visions of God. Uzziah was young and immature. He was likely prone to youthful impulsiveness. Even if he knew what to do, he might go about it wrong. But Zechariah would counsel him and help him do it right. All of us need someone strong in the Lord to speak into our lives. So many large churches are led by ministers who are isolated, and are accountable to no one. I beg you, if you are in such a church, get out.

Thirdly, we also see in verse 5 the condition of God's blessing. There it says that God made him to prosper. But before that it says "as long as he sought the Lord" and that's the condition. He was humble before God. He was so humble he only wanted God's will for himself. But there came a time in his late years, when his godly friend Zechariah was dead, that Uzziah no longer concerned himself with seeking the Lord. He became powerful and famous. That's when the tragedy of ungodly compromise ended his ministry. In verse 15, the Scripture says, "...his name spread far abroad; for he was marvelously helped, till he was strong." He lost his humility. Then verse 16 says "But when he was strong, his heart was lifted up to his destruction..." His humility was the condition of his blessing, and he forsook it.

Uzziah got *so used to being empowered, he started thinking he had the power.* He started using and abusing his position. We see many today who have lost their passion for God, and they are just operating out of their position. They should resign before they undo all the good things they have accomplished. Or, they should drop everything and rediscover that passion! God is calling and preparing hundreds of ministers on this campus. May God help us to help them have these three elements of godly prosperity: a passion for God's will; the influence of a godly friend, and the humility to stay with God. Somebody here needs to cut a path and leave a trail of blessing for their family, for their church, for their community, for their world.

Someone in your family is watching you now. They are waiting to see if your faith is real. Co-workers are observing how you walk as a Christian. You don't always know, but there are folk in your church watching you. They need to see a strong example of seeking the Lord. Neighbors are watching. You have an opportunity to lead them all in the right direction. You can seek the Lord in such a way that you "cut a path and blaze a trail" for them to come closer to God in their own lives. If you do that, then God will *empower* you. But never make the mistake Uzziah made and think that *you* have the power. Walk humbly and keep the blessings coming.

WISE PEOPLE GET WISER – DUMB GET DUMBER

"Give instruction to a wise man, and he will be yet wiser: teach a just man, and he will increase in learning. The fear of the LORD is the beginning of wisdom: and the knowledge of the Holy is understanding. For by me thy days shall be multiplied, and the years of thy life shall be increased." Proverbs 9:9-11

"Instead of dumbing down our youth we ought to smarten them up."

In the youth culture it is not fashionable to be wise. Those who attempt to speak properly and make good grades are ridiculed. State school systems repeatedly must lower the grading scale so that more students can make B's and qualify for a free pass to college. At the same time state colleges are pressured to lower the scores required on entrance exams. That's a process many have called the "dumbing down" of America.

This text says give instruction to a wise man and he will be yet wiser. Proverbs 1:5 says a wise man will hear and will increase learning. God's Word puts a premium on wisdom. The wise man built his house upon a rock. The wise virgins had extra oil in their lamps. Proverbs 22:17-24:17 were written by a group of people called "the wise men." There are numerous references to the contrast between wise and foolish people throughout the Bible. Verse 11 of our text actually says that wisdom will make you live longer – it will add years to your life! How do you become wise? Well, there is a definite starting point. It is stated in verse 10: "The fear of the Lord is the beginning of wisdom..." The example of the wise men in the Christmas story takes it from there. First, they had a goal: to find Jesus. That required movement, travel. That required a determined effort. That required persistent inquiry.

Second, they had gifts: gold and myrrh and frankincense. The gold could have been a gift for a human king. The myrrh, itself worth its own weight in gold, could have been a gift for a great physician. But the frankincense was either a gift to a High Priest, or it was burnt as an act of worship to a deity. The gifts meant they knew who Jesus was! Third, they had guidance. When they came they were guided by a star. Today we are guided by the Spirit. When they had found Jesus, they went back a different way, being told to do so by God in a dream. That kept them from walking into Herod's trap and being killed or imprisoned. The guidance of the Spirit is a wonderful blessing to keep us out of the traps of the devil.

More than likely if you are reading this book, you already believe in God. You know He created Heaven and earth and that one day you will be brought into account before Him. It is good that you already have a healthy respect for your Creator. But have you met the Son of God Jesus Christ and made Him your Saviour and your Lord? Giving your soul to Jesus is the beginning of true wisdom. But it's just a beginning! Have you given your best gift to him? What is the most valuable thing you have besides your soul? Your time! You're just allotted so much time here on earth, and then you will be in Eternity. How are you using your time? Are you being led by the Spirit now? He will lead you to wisdom. And once you get some, you will want more. And one day someone will remember something you once told them – and say, "A wise person once told me…" It's good to be wise. It's dumb to be dumb. The Spirit of God led you here. You are already wise, but you will become wiser still. And that will lengthen your days on earth. It's good to pray that you may be known as a wise man or wise woman.

A BEGINNING WITH NO END

"Thus saith God the LORD, he that created the heavens, and stretched them out; he that spread forth the earth, and that which cometh out of it; he that giveth breath unto the people upon it, and spirit to them that walk therein." Isaiah 42:5

"God created us and now supplies our bodies with breath and our souls with spirit. But why?"

We have all wondered, at least when we were still young and inquisitive, why we were put here. It's a child's natural question: "Where did I come from?" And usually it is coupled with, Why?" Where *did* we come from? For what reason? To know the reason for being is life's greatest question. But we must be very careful about the attitude in which we ask this question. Only those who ask in the proper humility of a creature approaching its own Creator will ever know the answer.

This chapter is the beginning of a new section of Isaiah, where the Holy Spirit takes us to a higher perspective and gives us glimpse of God's view of the starry heavens and earth. Here in verse 5 we are given a cosmic picture. In my mind's eye I am looking down on the solar system – the blazing central star we call the sun, with all the gleaming planets in orbit, and various moons in orbit around the planets. In the background of the solar system are millions of glittering galaxies laid out like a winter scene of sparkling snow and ice. God says he did that. He made the heavens out of nothing (the Hebrew word *bara* means exactly that). Then he stretched them forth. In fact, science tells us that the universe is still expanding! And God said he hammered out the earth. The Hebrew word *raqa* here indicates the skilled work of a master craftsman who spreads out a precious metal by beating it. It tells us God was preparing something of great value for himself. Why did he make the earth?

In verse 5 he describes mankind as the central reason for creating the earth. Why did he make mankind? He states clearly that he is the one that gives people breath, (in Hebrew *neshamah*). In Acts 17:25 we are reminded by Paul that God is the one who gives us breath and life. Acts 17:28 says that in him we move and have our being. Breathing is what biology tells us is an involuntary movement. Our diaphragm has been programmed by God to expand and contract on its own. It works even when we are asleep. So do the heart muscles. But only as long as God wills them to do so. Why does God keep you alive?

Here's another question: Why did he give you a spirit? Not only does he give us breath, but he gives us the human spirit that other animals do not have. In Proverbs 20:27 it is called the candle of the Lord. So, what is God up to? Why did he make us? Why are we equipped with a spirit? Acts 17:27 says he did it so that we would seek him and find him. Revelation 4:11 says we were created for his pleasure. We were designed for fellowship with God. In order to do that we must be made as eternal spirits. We had a beginning but we will have no end. But we must also be holy, for without holiness no man shall see God. It is through the spirit that we are made holy. Why does he give us a spirit and why does he want to make us holy?

God made us with free moral choice so that our love for him would be like his love for us – a free choice. Our first use of that choice was to sin against God. But with that choice we can choose the offer of redemption made to us by Jesus, God's son. And through union with his holy spirit we can grow in holiness. Out of that holiness we can serve the Lord here and fellowship with him in eternity. *That is why we are here: why you were born, why you were saved, why you were called, and why you are now here training for godly life and ministry!*

You cannot have his companionship in eternity if he cannot have yours now. My question to you today is: "How concerned are you with becoming holy?" It is why you were made, and why God has spared your life, and why he has called you. You cannot have a ministry without being holy. You dare not die without being holy. Let's make that our prayer focus today.

DANCING WITH BROKEN BONES

"Make me to hear joy and gladness; that the bones which thou has broken my rejoice." Psalms 51:8

"As you grow in the Lord you will reach a point where you will receive so much joy that you will even celebrate times when you fell and injured yourself and your ministry. You will even rejoice over the experiences God used to break you and discipline you."

Philip Keller in his best-seller, *A Shepherd Looks at Psalm 23*, tells about a practice by the shepherds in the Mid-East. He says that sometimes an orphan lamb gets too reckless and wanders away from his view too much. When that happens, the shepherd will break one of the lamb's legs, set it, and then carry the bandaged lamb from place to place until it is healed again. In this manner, the lamb becomes completely dependent upon the shepherd: for water, for grazing, for protection. When his bones heal, he will be one of the sheep that sticks closest to the shepherd.

In Psalm 51:8, we see David praying for forgiveness after he has committed adultery and murder. He has already been chastened by Nathan the prophet. He is suffering heavy conviction and a great sense of loss of fellowship with God. He feels like his bones have been broken. He wants joy and gladness again. The word for rejoice here is interesting. It is *sámah* – usually a burst of emotion that results in singing or dancing. Some translators use the word dance. What a thought! David wants his broken bones to dance again!

But that is a great metaphor to adequately describe the joy of complete restoration! Most of us here have been injured by ourselves, by others, or had to be chastened by God. We've got some broken bones. But we can be forgiven, restored, and made better than ever! That's God's plan for you. Those broken bones will be healed. The world, the flesh nature, and the Devil all want you to give up on ever getting back to where you could have been with God. They want you to accept your brokenness and resign yourself to a life of sadness over "what might have been." But God wants you to look to a bright future, when your broken bones will dance with joy!

There is a suffering in the flesh that is caused by our own sinful foolishness. But learning the hard lessons of brokenness and getting godly sorrow can lead to true repentance, forgiveness and complete restoration. When you have been through all that, you are never again attracted to that thing that snared you before. As the Word of God says in I Peter 4:1, "FOR AS MUCH then as Christ hath suffered for us in the flesh, arm yourselves likewise with the same mind: for he that hath suffered in the flesh hath ceased from sin:" Living more holy leads to living in more blessings. Truly, you will come to a time of such joy in your life, that you will want to dance with the very bones that were once so broken!

ARE YOU "FAR" OR "NEAR?"

"For, lo, they that are far from thee shall perish: thou hast destroyed all them that go a whoring from thee. But it is good for me to draw near to God: I have put my trust in the Lord GOD, that I may declare all thy works." Psalm 73:27-28

"It is possible to falsely assume you are a Christian. The only safe theology starts and ends with the Presence of God in your life."

Asaph, the song writer, was concerned with the prosperity of the wicked. They did not seem to have any troubles, while all day long he was plagued and chastened. He became so envious, he almost slipped spiritually. But God showed him that the prosperity of the wicked was just a set-up. They would one day be brought down in a moment and be utterly consumed with terrors. Then he shares a wonderful revelation with us in verses 23-28. He lays hold on four great truths. First, he has God's Presence, v. 23. Second, he realizes his true Preference, v. 25. Third, he knows God Himself is all the Provision he needs, v. 26. Fourth, he has a Profession, v. 28. In this fourth great declaration, there is a progression of three steps.

In verse 28a he sees it has been good to draw near to God. In 28b he knows he has put his trust in the Lord GOD. And in 28c he knows that his purpose in life is to declare all of God's works. But the most striking thing about this passage is the contrast that one makes between the wicked in verse 27, and himself, in verse 28. Here we see the words, "far" and "near" contrasted. Those that are "far" from God will perish. Those that are near to God will be able to trust him and speak of His works in their own life. So now we come to the main thrust of this passage. There is safety in a working relationship with God. Do you really have one?

In 2 Corinthians we are told to "examine ourselves, whether we be in the faith;" Some denominations have drawn up the following four tests by which a man may examine himself and test the reality of his Christianity. First, do you know salvation through the Cross of Christ? Second, are you growing in the power of the Holy Spirit, in prayer, meditation and the knowledge of God? Third, is there a great desire to spread the Kingdom of God by example, and by preaching and teaching? Fourth, are you bringing others to Christ by individual conversations, and by public witness?

When I was thirteen, I attended a revival service in a rural church where the visiting preacher was describing the fate of the lost. For the first time, I heard about how awful hell would be. When the altar invitation was given I found myself responding – along with several other children. I was afraid not to go. And it was a very emotional experience. My own family was not very demonstrative. We just didn't cry. But when elderly women came up and hugged me with tears in their eyes, I began to weep. That alone convinced me that I had been saved.

But as I recall, in the days following I felt no new nearness to God, I had no new love for Christ, and the same old mean streak inside me kept manifesting itself. Yet for the next three or four years, I thought I was saved. God was merciful, and kept me from getting killed, or I would have fallen straight into the pits of hell. It was only in my late teens that I realized I was still lost. I began to run with the wrong crowd and get into trouble with the law. It dawned on me in one of several jails where I was taken against my will that I was not saved. It was then, while reading a Gideon New Testament that I truly gave my heart and life to the Lord. He then took the broken, twisted wreckage of my life and made me over again.

We don't have to answer for the conscience of others who profess Christianity, but we do have to make sure our own Christianity is real – not a masquerade. There are, however, some people around you that need to see some real Christianity, so that they will want to abandon their own counterfeit faith for one that is real! We must let our lights shine in all the dark corners. And we must be the salt that makes others thirsty for Christ! You cannot be salt and light if you are far from Christ. Determine today to walk closer to Him.

S P I R I T U A L   W E L L   D I G G E R S

"Blessed is the man whose strength is in thee; in whose heart are the ways of them. Who passing through the valley of Baca make it a well; the rain also filleth the pools." Psalm 84:5-6

"There are special Christians who know how to use their own troubles to help others."

Each of us will eventually find ourselves occasionally in a dry place. What a blessing it would be if in those times we knew someone who had been there ahead of us and could speak into our lives. One day we ourselves will be the one who has been there before someone following us. The question then will be: did we leave a well for them? Bacah is the word which indicates a very dry place. Only balsam trees will grow there. The psalmist here is describing the heart of a pilgrim who must pass through such a valley. Instead of conserving all his energy and water to just make it through – the pilgrim stops and digs a well so that it will be easier for others to come that way! Think about that!

It is hot. He may dehydrate. It may take him an extra day. He may use up his own water jar and just desperately hope that he finds water at the bottom of this well. But his work is not for himself, else he would keep moving. It is for *others*. But this is more about spiritual ministry that it is about digging a physical well. Verse 5 says that blessed is the man whose strength is in God, and who has in his heart the ways of this pilgrim. Let's list those ways. First, there must be a strong devotional base, verses 1-5. Second, this must be someone who is able to "pass through," verse 6. Some people never get past their own problems to consider the needs of others.

Third, they are focused on others, verse 6. Someone already passing through would only dig a well for others. Fourth, they know how to bring blessing no matter where they are, verse 6. They will turn any dry place into a well. When they do that, God adds his blessing and creates additional pools of water. The whole landscape changes. Fifth, they continue to grow spiritually, verse 7. Sixth, they have a positive attitude. They start with sand, but believe that if they keep digging they will find water. Seventh, they know a great secret, verse 11 and 12. No good thing will God withhold from them who walk uprightly!

How does one dig a well for others while going through a difficult time? Here are some ideas: keep a prayer journal and share your experience later. Find someone traveling at the same time through the same valley and to share your secret with them. Or, let people see how you deal with your difficulty with a strong faith in God. Or, let your experience give you a place of intercession so that you know how to pray for those who face the same valley. Or, develop a set of lessons you learned that you can now teach others. What are you doing with your dry valley? Pray that God will use you to make it better for someone else! That's the Jesus way!

THE LORD CAN AFFORD TO WAIT, BUT CAN YOU?

"And therefore will the LORD wait, that he may be gracious unto you, and therefore will he be exalted, that he may have mercy upon you: for the LORD is a God of judgment: blessed are all they that wait for him." Isaiah 30:18

"When we are in trouble, we can come up with man-made and man-centered plans to get ourselves out of trouble. God will just

wait until we have exhausted every one and are ready to wholly depend upon him."

The country of Judah was in trouble. The military super-power of Assyria had already destroyed the northern king-dom of Israel and now threatened Judah. Isaiah said they should trust only in God. But the leaders hastily made an alliance with Egypt, another superpower. So God says in verse 17 that they were going to be attacked until they were left as only a small surviving outpost, like a signal fire on a far-away mountain.

In verse 18, God says that he will just wait so that He may be gracious to the survivors. When He is exalted then he will have mercy on them. The last line of the verse says, "Blessed are all they that wait for Him." Isaiah's message was this: God can afford to wait, but can you? Is this a word for you? You've gotten yourself into a bit of a bind, so you've started making some plans. Is it a loan? An extra job? Or getting married to someone with a good job? Are you already working on plan "B?" Selling your house or car? Or just dropping out of college?

Hear me: God wants to be gracious and merciful to you. But He will wait until you exhaust all your self-made plans in failure. God alone is your hope. God alone deserves glory for what you accomplish here. Listen! You can be mightily blessed! Just learn to wait for God to act. My family and I were struggling financially due to my extended illness. I had bought a home on property adjoining mine. I thought it was a good plan. I would rent it out, and the extra income would help us survive. But the renter turned out to be a con-artist. Really! Years later I saw his face on television as the FBI was looking for him.

At the time however, I thought he was a Christian. So I got the first month's rent payment. The next few were delayed, and finally they stopped coming. I got into real trouble financially. I was in danger of losing both homes. Then I cried out to God as my only hope. I was able to sell the property and God got me out of a mess I had created. Whatever it is that you are trying to work out – it is best to surrender it back to God. You may think you're waiting on God when you really aren't. You're pushing ahead, trying to make it all work out. But He's waiting for you to show your total dependence upon Him. You're waiting for your plans to work out. Tell me, who can best afford to wait a long, long time?

This is a life lesson that seems to be so hard to learn that most of us go through the lesson experience God arranges for us again and again before we finally get it. Let's pray for more wisdom in this area. It is so easy for parents to think they are the best parents in the world and know exactly how to solve a parenting problem. It is so easy to fall into the trap of thinking we are financial wizards and can get ourselves out of any financial pinch. But sooner or later we must learn to take everything to God in prayer, and to wait on His answer no matter how long it takes!

THE GREAT EXCHANGE

"To appoint unto them that mourn in Zion, to give unto them beauty for ashes, the oil of joy for mourning, the garment of praise for the spirit of heaviness; that they might be called trees of righteousness, the planting of the LORD, that he might be glorified." Isaiah 61:3

"In shopping, when you get something that doesn't work, you take it back for an exchange. What about your life?"

God gave Isaiah some good news here. Jesus quoted part of it when He began His ministry in Nazareth. You can go to God to exchange ashes for beauty, mourning for joy, and heaviness for praise! The kind of beauty here is actually the majestic trappings of royalty, and the kind of joy is a rejoicing that overcomes grief. This kind of praise survives all kinds of heaviness. What a great exchange! Some notable persons in the Bible who made this great exchange are Saul of Tarsus, the Prodigal Son, the Thief on the Cross. Those were able to make the great exchange because God had already made an even greater exchange. On Calvary He gave His Son Jesus' blood – in exchange for your soul!

All of us have known what it is to sit in the ashes of great ambitions and dreams. But God comes and through the exchange at the Cross, you can have the beauty of holiness – as a member of the royal family of God! We have all had times of grief and mourning – especially when we part with a loved one. But God turns mourning into the joyful hope of the Resurrection. All of us have been depressed, but God can put a song in your heart. When something you bought doesn't work, you either take it back where you bought it and make an exchange, or you buy something to replace it. Our lives were not working, so we went to God and made the great exchange and got a new life!

My life at age 18 was all fouled up. Rebellious, angry, and mean, I got away from home and got arrested, several times. The kind of friends I had did not help me. The entertainment I sought did not make me happy. Alcoholic drink did not bring relief. Then I realized one night in a New Orleans jail that my life was all used up. I saw myself in the faces of the older inmates. I was becoming like them. Now I could never find a good wife – who would have me? I could never have a respectable job – who would hire me? I had not only ruined my own life, but I had broken my mother's heart, and brought shame upon my family.

I contemplated suicide, even planning how I might do it. My life was over. But then I began to read some Scripture, John 3:16. I was perishing, but Jesus died on the cross that I might not perish, but have everlasting life. What a great exchange! That night I gave Jesus my broken, used up life, and He gave me a brand new one. I have never been sorry I made the exchange. I have true happiness and peace. My negative mind has been changed and I think positive things now. My life is filled with the goodness of God. From that moment, my life took a new course. I got out of jail and went straight. I got baptized, joined a church, and started serving God. I had a weight taken off my heart, and I had new thoughts in my mind. God started working things out for good in my life. I started testifying and preaching. I entered the ministry and became a pastor. God turned it all around and gave me a great new life!

Do you have this "beauty for ashes, oil of joy for mourning, garment of praise for heaviness?" If you do, you ought to be one of the happiest people on earth! Nobody can make a better exchange than that! But right now you may be thinking of someone who has lost it all, wasted every opportunity, and whose life is in ruins today. Perhaps you should share my story with them. They may be ready to make the great exchange too!

MADE, MARRED, MADE AGAIN

"And the vessel that he made of clay was marred in the hand of the potter: so he made it again another vessel, as seemed good to the potter to make it." Jeremiah 18:4

"Any person who starts out in ministry has been marred, or "messed up." A minister is of no use to God until he or she is made again."

In Jeremiah 18 we have the story in which God sends Jeremiah to the potter's house for an object lesson. That lesson is for all of us. Jeremiah saw the potter make a jar. Then it became marred, so it was necessary to make it again – into an entirely different vessel than before. The words "made, marred, and made again" appear together in verse 4. The word for "made" used twice in verse 4 and also in verse 6 the word for "do" is the word "asah". "Asah" was first used in Genesis 1:26, where we read, "And God said, Let us make man in our image..." So God designed and made us in His own image.

But then there is the word "marred." It is the word that first appeared in Genesis 6: "shawkath," which means to ruin, violate, injure, wound, or mar. That is what Satan has done to each of us. Most of these injuries persist even after the new birth, and there is emotional damage, or clouded minds, or soulish attitudes. In verse 6, God asks, "O house of Israel, cannot I do with you as this potter? Saith the Lord, Behold, as the clay is in mine hand, so are ye in mine hand, O house of Israel." So it is obvious that God is the potter in this picture, and we are the clay.

We all came into the ministry with flaws. But these were not "design flaws." They are the results of damage by sin. So every one of us must go back to the factory, so to speak. We were made by God, and then marred, and now we must be made again. My own life is a perfect example. When God called me into ministry, I had just been saved in a jail. I was in no shape to minister to anybody. I had to be made all over again. The process took years, and in some very real ways is still going on. I'm still being changed.

From the perspective of the clay, the process is not pleasant. We must be completely broken down again and thrown back on the wheel. There we spin around and around, getting nowhere in ministry, but going through a life-changing personal process. While we are going around and around, we feel the heavy hand of the Potter, squeezing us and reshaping us. We become humble, soft, and pliant. We have no say in what we are becoming. The Potter will make us into another vessel, as it seems good to the Potter to make us. This is not a quick fix. The process may use up the majority of our years on earth. But when the Potter is finished, we will be fit for the Master's use. And then we will have our greatest years!

You are here, many of you, in the midst of the first phase of the process. You may seem to be going around and around, getting nowhere. You may feel a heavy hand upon your life. But be thankful. It means God has great plans for you. You were made by God, you have been marred, but praise God, He is making you again! Don't let any critical and demeaning remarks of others get to you. You were marred all right. There's no debate about that. Some of those who put you down as worthless are themselves marred, and as yet, their own remaking process has not started. But the wonderful secret you enjoy is that the Potter is making you a totally new vessel. Just smile and wait and see what God will do with you!

GOD'S GOT THE PLAN

"For I know the thoughts that I think toward you, saith the

LORD, thoughts of peace, and not of evil, to give you an expected end." Jeremiah 29:11

"Sometimes, your plans must be interrupted by God's plan."

The nation of Judah had been destroyed by Babylonia. Most of the people were taken away captive to Babylonia. God has Jeremiah write them a letter to encourage them. In the previous verse, God has already told these captives that they will be there seventy years. Then he will bring them back to Judah. Now he tells them that it's all part of a plan for their good. The Jews had falsely believed that their nation would never fall. After all, they had the Temple of the God of the universe. So, they went about their plans as usual, even though Nebuchadnezzar had made two previous invasions against them. They didn't repent of their sins and beg God for mercy.

So, God allowed the captivity. He interrupted their plans. They lost their homes, their businesses, and their money. But he says in verse 11, "I know the thoughts that I think toward you, saith the Lord, thoughts of peace, and not of evil, to give you an expected end." This word "end" is from "achariyth," and means after, or following this, or the future. God has a plan for your future! The principle here is this: God allows unpleasant experiences to interrupt our plans, so that we will be ready to follow his plan. Following his plan, our lives work out far better. God says that his thoughts for us are of peace and not evil. He wants you to receive the expected end – his blessings on your life.

That's what happened with the first church in Jerusalem. They all knew what Jesus had told them to do. They were to make disciples in Jerusalem, then Judea and Samaria, then the uttermost parts of the earth. But they all had jobs and businesses there in Jerusalem. They were unwilling to travel or to relocate. So God allowed persecution to break out. Then in Acts 8:1 says they were all scattered abroad in the regions of Judea and Samaria.

Furthermore, Acts 8:4 says "Therefore they that were scattered abroad went every where preaching the word!" Imagine that! God had interrupted their plans so that they would follow his. I had plans to build a great church in Covington, Georgia. But God interrupted my plans with Lupus. He allowed it because I was so hard-headed he couldn't get my attention any other way. Then he healed me and gave me a renewed call to the teaching ministry. And now I am following his plan and finding more joy and satisfaction in my life than ever before! What are you planning? Is it really God's plan for your life? Perhaps your plans have already been interrupted. That's why you are here at this college! God has some great thoughts about you. As you read this, you may realize that your own plans are constantly meeting with failure. Could this be a hint that God has something much greater in mind for you?

DO YOU FEEL THE
TUG OF THE CURRENT?

"Afterward, he measured a thousand; and it was a river that I could not pass over: for the waters were risen, waters to swim in, a river that could not be passed over." Ezekiel 47: 5

"The Holy Spirit is like this river. You can wade in ankle deep if you want to. But you will experience very little of His power until you go all the way and commit yourself to the depth of the river and the pull of its powerful current."

Early in my ministry I discovered that my preaching was effective enough get people to commit to Christ, but it didn't seem to have enough effect to produce changed lives. So I read every book I could get on the filling of the Holy Spirit. I wanted His power in my preaching. But that desire didn't take me far enough into the river. I needed the power of the Holy Spirit for my whole life! You may feel that's where you are now: not deep enough! Let's look at this passage and see what God will speak into your heart.

In this vision Ezekiel is given some very precise measurements of the river. He and the angel measure the river from where it starts for exactly 4,000 cubits. After every measurement of 1000 cubits, Ezekiel is brought through the waters to test its depth. When the trickle has run only 1000 cubits, it covers his ankles. When it has gone 2000 cubits, it covers his knees. When it has gone 3000, it is up to his loins. When it has gone 4000, it is too deep to wade. The phrase "river that could not be passed over" is repeated for emphasis in verse 5.

That means that the stream becomes a mighty "white water" cascade of current in just one mile! This passage is highly symbolic, because each stage of the river's depth represents a measurement of your involvement with the Holy Spirit! The feet and ankles are a picture of our outward walk – observable behavior. That's the first thing that changes when we receive the Spirit of Christ into our lives. And we don't change much without the power of that Spirit.

The knees represent a prayer life. As we get deeper into the river, our prayer life changes and becomes far more effectual. The loins are the biblical symbol of strength and ability to reproduce. When we go deeper, we become strong enough to have a consistent testimony through trials and temptations. And we are able to make disciples, or reproduce spiritually. Notice, however, that at all three of these levels we are still wading. We can cross over and get out whenever we please. And we often do.

However, when we are in the waters as we should be, we are no longer wading. Wading allows you to go where you want to go. But we are committed to the current when we swim in white water. We cannot cross and get out on the other side - we can only swim with the current. That's when the Holy Spirit affects our entire lives. When I finally understood that I didn't just need an anointing to preach, but I needed it to live holy and please God, I started swimming in the current. And my work began to be effective – I started having fruit that remains! You will too. Just commit yourself to the current. You already feel the tug!

HOW MUCH SPIRITUAL "REBAR" DO YOU NEED?

"But Daniel purposed in his heart that he would not defile himself with the portion of the king's meat, nor with the wine which he drank: therefore he requested of the prince of the eunuchs that he might not defile himself." Daniel 1:8

"Living in today's pagan society is like having a house made of concrete in an earthquake zone. If you don't have any rebar in that concrete, you're going to lose everything."

This verse says that Daniel "purposed in his heart" that he would not yield to the pressure of his surroundings and defile himself before God. That word in Hebrew is "suwn" and it means to "put something somewhere." His determination was like reinforcement iron bars for concrete – what we call "rebar."

The background to his determination is this. He was taken captive in his teens and brought to a pagan country. Because he was of the royal family, he was selected for re-education in Chaldean thought patterns. That is what is meant in verse 4, where we read "whom they might teach the learning and the tongue of the Chaldeans." His Hebrew name, Daniel, meant "God is my Judge." But he was forced to take on a new name as part of his brainwashing. The new name meant "May Bel protect his life" – a reference to a pagan deity.

The pressure of worldliness and temptation on Christians in this society is about as bad as it was in the days of Daniel. If we are going to survive spiritually, we must "put something somewhere" inside us so that we won't crumble like concrete in an earthquake. The earthquakes are already shaking the foundations of Christian family life. Our own country is fully pagan. This is one of the few countries where homosexual marriages are being sanctioned by law. We kill a million healthy babies per year as a means of birth control. There is a concerted effort to remove any notion of God in our culture. Regular programming on television defiles the mind with pornographic scenes and filthy expletives. Legal efforts are underway to remove "under God" from the pledge of allegiance, to take away the Ten Commandments from all public buildings, to remove "in God we trust" from our currency.

As we follow the story of Daniel, we find that he not only survived, but he overcame the pagan culture around him. He rose to prominence and influenced the whole empire for good. The first king, Nebuchadnezzar got saved and gave his testimony in Chapter 4. When the Persians took over, King Darius decreed that throughout his empire people should fear the God of Daniel. That's because Daniel purposed something in his heart. It was a conscious decision. He drew a line and determined not to cross it. God saw that and helped him. God is looking at our hearts. Do we need to put some spiritual rebar in our hearts? If not now, when?

WHERE IN YOUR LIFE DO YOU PROVE YOUR FAITH IN GOD?

"And the LORD answered me, and said, Write the vision, and make it plain upon tables, that he may run that readeth it. For the vision is yet for an appointed time, but at the end it shall speak, and not lie: though it tarry, wait for it; because it will surely come, it will not tarry. Behold, his soul which is lifted up is not upright in him; but the just shall live by his faith." Habakkuk 2:2-4

"We are called to be visionaries – that's what leaders are; but faith is required for a vision."

We have the definition of personal faith in Hebrews 11:1. It is the substance of things hoped for, the evidence of things not seen. Hebrews 11:6 tells us that without faith it is impossible to please God. The Bible teaches that we are saved by grace through faith, we please God by faith, and we live by faith. That's what faith is and what faith does.

It also helps if we know what is not faith. It cannot be what you can see. It cannot be faith if you understand it. It cannot be faith if you can learn it. It cannot be faith if you can do it by yourself. It cannot be foolishness – like obligating yourself for an expensive car you cannot afford just to keep up appearances. It must be a manner of trusting God for something he has already approved; that is already tangible and real to you. So I ask the question again, "Where in your life do you demonstrate your faith in God?"

Faith is first tested in small steps. Before Elijah called down fire from heaven on Mt. Carmel, he witnessed daily miracles in his life for three years. Before big financial miracles must come miracles of daily provision. When you're down to your last five dollars, and God tells you to give it away – could you do it? Can you trust God to provide for gas to get to work, or for milk and bread tomorrow?

We are surrounded by role models who don't have to trust God for anything. They draw such huge salaries, they never have to take any personal steps of faith in the financial area. Yet they consider themselves experts on faith teaching. Before you teach it you should live it. More is caught than taught. Take the area of missions. Most church members in this country have never been overseas on a mission for Christ. They can't see how they can come up with the money for the trip. Years ago, when I was a church planter, I would always start with no set salary. But God would provide for my family and all the bills would be paid.

We learned to be very careful with the tithe. It was not ours. And we learned to give, even the last cash we had at times. And God always provided. I felt led to overseas missions. I started using all my vacation allotment to go on short term missions to places like Costa Rica and Mexico. The cost came out of my own pocket or from friends. God always provided – sometimes at the very last moment. By using our faith every day, we began to just know that where God guides, he provides.

Before you can be a world class ambassador for the Lord Jesus, you must learn to prove your faith. Sometimes a trip costs thousands of dollars. But it's God's bill if it's his will. You will receive the provision, but you must be careful not to spend it for anything else, even though you have real needs. You may have to build up your faith to the point that God can trust you with his provision. There are probably faith tests presenting themselves to you right now. God wants you to practice your faith. God is a rewarder of them who believe that he is, and that he rewards those who seek him.

Check it out. Where in your life are you proving your faith in God? Are you stepping out on faith alone to attempt to do something you know God has directed you to do? Are you waiting on God and no one else for something big in your life? If someone was watching your example, what would they learn about faith? Some preachers teach on faith when they really get all their own needs met by letting them be known to a sympathetic congregation! Let's get away from placing our faith in the sympathy of others, and learn to trust God alone! If you are believing God for the price of a ticket, try just telling God and no one else! Practice your faith daily and it will grow daily.

Part Two
SOME NEW TESTAMENT
LIFE LESSONS

I FOUND NO MONUMENT AT CALVARY

"And when they were come to the place, which is called Calvary, there they crucified him, and the malefactors, one on the right hand, and the other on the left." Luke 23:33

"Considering how the event at Calvary has influenced so much history, you'd expect to find a huge marble monument at the spot. And there should be spotlights to light it up at night. Exactly what is there to see now? I am one of only a few people who even know what it looks like today."

More than thirty times I have stood at the foot of the hill called Calvary, just outside the old city of Jerusalem. At its base is a beautiful garden of trees, shrubs and flowers. At one end of the garden, closest to the place where the crosses once stood, is a small platform with steps and rails. At the other end of the garden, about 100 yards away, is the Empty Tomb. Many times I led groups of pilgrims on a visit to this garden. But we were never allowed to go up on the hill of Calvary. A Moslem cemetery is there behind a locked and guarded gate. Christians are not allowed.

But on an occasion in 1969, a Moslem friend escorted me inside that gate and he and I climbed the hill of Calvary. My friend was Mr. Sinokrot, the owner of the Rivoli Hotel. The back of the hotel stood against the cemetery fence. When we reached the summit, we found on the bald granite summit three round sockets cut into the rock. Each was about 8 inches wide and 20 inches deep. It was here that the Romans once publicly crucified lawbreakers as a lesson to others. The crosses once stood in these sockets, like signposts, overlooking the busy Damascus highway.

God had marked this spot in history long before Jesus hung here on the cross. Over 2,000 years before the crucifixion of Jesus, on the slope just below this spot, God had brought Abraham and Isaac to enact what became a prophetic picture of what God and His Son would do in this place (Genesis 22). When God provided a perfect sacrificial animal so that Isaac could be spared, Abraham broke into prophecy and named the place "Jehovah Jireh." He went on to announce, "In this mountain of the Lord, it shall be seen," meaning that what had just transpired would be seen again in the future. Over 1,000 years before the crucifixion of Jesus, God had brought David to a flat rock on the same slope. Here David purchased a threshing floor from a Jebusite to become the site of an altar, and later to be used as the location of the Temple. When David made his offering at this location, God accepted the offering and spared the people from a great plague. This too was a picture of God accepting the sacrifice of Jesus and sparing us from the plague and curse of sin.

It was here that the sinless Jesus Christ was crucified in the place of all who have broken the law of God. And on that cold April day with sleet stinging my face, I cried and prayed while my Moslem friend bowed his head in respect. This is the place where we can see man at his worst and God at his best. The place where God blessed and a mob cursed. This is the place where you can feel the awful depth of human sin, and the tremendous height of God's love. It's where all history was changed, and time itself was divided into BC and AD.

There is no marker. It is just as well. What monument could possibly be magnificent enough? But there should be a marker in every human life. A monument to God's grace – to His compassion and deliverance from darkness and hell. What's there in your life to serve as a memorial to what Jesus did on Calvary?

THE OTHER SIDE OF THE PASSION

"To whom also he shewed himself alive after his passion by many infallible proofs, being seen of them forty days, and speaking of the things pertaining to the kingdom of God." Acts 1:3

"The Passion of Christ was neither the beginning nor the end of the story. Wait until you hear the rest of the story! About the other side of the Passion!"

On March 6, 2004 I saw a film that I won't ever forget. It started with the agony of Jesus in the Garden of Gethsemane and ends with the empty grave cloths. It was entirely about the unbelievable torture Jesus endured on the last night and day of his life on earth. The film opened with Jesus saying, "If it be possible, let this cup pass from me." His body shook as he struggled in anguish to settle his resolve to go on with his awesome plan to allow himself to be crucified. He was dealing with all his fully human emotions and dreading the ordeal he faced. He knew precisely what he would have to undergo. Yet because of His passion to die in my place and redeem me, he endured it all.

The film was director Mel Gibson's labor of love – an effort to show as never before the violent, brutal, wicked treatment Jesus endured for all of us. It was appropriately titled, "The Passion." Passion is a strong word, but it fits and it is biblical. Webster's says it is any powerful emotion, like love or hate. But the English word "passion" itself comes from the Latin meaning to suffer, and came into the English language because of the suffering of Christ. Whatever you are passionate about is your passion, and you are willing to suffer for it. And there will never be a greater example that than of Christ. Acts 1:3 uses the phrase, "after his passion." Yes, there is an "after." I would like to share with you what I call the "Other Side of the Passion." But since we have an "after," we must also have a "before." And we find that in the plan of God, there was a "before," and there is an "after" to the Passion. Let me share briefly with you four phases that are clearly shown in the Bible – the rest of the story!

First, there was *Compassion*. God the Father, God the Spirit and God the Son saw our helpless condition. The Father said, "I love them." The Son had compassion and said, "I will go and redeem them." The Spirit said, "I will go and help you bring them back to the Father." Second, there was *Compulsion*. Jesus came into to the world to go to the cross. The Devil tried to stop him after his birth, after his baptism, and then before the cross. Nothing would stop him. He faced the cross, driven by the compulsion of his compassion. Third, there was the *Completion*. He went through the Passion to complete his work to complete us! The work could not stop with anything less than suffering for the sins of the whole world. It could not stop with anything less than the offering of his sinless blood as the one perfect sacrifice. It would not even be complete without his death. Fourth, there was the *Commotion*. When he died, the sky went black and the earth shook. But three days later something happened that has been shaking the world ever since. He got up again. He proved himself alive again, by many infallible proofs! The other side of the Passion brings us into a head-on encounter with the undeniable truth of a Living Saviour, Lord of Heaven and Earth. Fully able to deliver us and make us one with the Father!

The other side of the Passion is the Gospel! Seeing the film changed something inside me. I can never be silent about what Jesus did when there is a chance to speak. I have been entrusted with the Gospel. "Gospel" means "good news." The good news to everyone: you don't have to die in your sins. What a wonderful job! It's better than being a fireman and leading people out of the smoke and flames of a burning house. It's better than being a ship's captain who comes along side a sinking ship and saves people from drowning. I have been called to work on the other side of the Passion!

Telling people, "You can be saved!" That's the other side of the Passion.

STARTING A RIOT ABOUT JESUS

"When Jesus came into the coasts of Caesarea Philippi, he asked his disciples, saying, Whom do men say that I the Son of man am? And they said, Some say that thou art John the Baptist: some, Elias; and others, Jeremias, or one of the prophets. He saith unto them, But whom say ye that I am? And Simon Peter answered and said, Thou art the Christ, the Son of the living God." Matthew 16:13-16

"Being a Christian is not about the kind of person I think I am. It is about who I think Jesus is."

Preaching on this text, I caused a riot in Tanzania. In a local Assembly of God in the large coastal city of Dar Es Salaam , I spoke on the two questions Jesus asked. The first was "Whom do men say that I, the Son of man, am?" And four answers were reported: John the Baptist, Elijah, Jeremiah, or one of the prophets. I pointed out that this was what the Muslims were saying about Jesus. They say he is a prophet, but not as great a prophet as Mohammed. The second question that Jesus asked in this passage was "But whom say ye that I am?" I went on to point out that the answer Peter gave was revealed by the Spirit and confirmed by Jesus: "Thou are the Christ, the

Son of the Living God." Jesus is divine. He is part of the Godhead: God the Father, God the Son, God the Holy Spirit. Jesus is God. But Muslims say he is not God. In the face of what others are saying about Jesus – we must affirm that he is God.

This message was broadcast by radio. I returned to Nairobi the same day. After I left, a riot broke out in the streets of Dar Es Salaam. The Muslims marched through an area, burning cars and smashing windows. They were chanting, "Jesus is not God! Jesus is not God! Jesus is not God!" The message had struck a sore nerve in Islamic theology. It is the central issue between Islam and Christianity. We are surrounded in society by those who have various degrees of respect for Jesus, and who accord him at least some small place in their religion. Usually they concede that he was a great teacher, or a prophet, or at least a very good man. You can get along with these practitioners of other religions as long as you don't dispute their claims. But if you begin to assert that Jesus is far more than they claim – that he is in fact Lord of all; then you will begin to cause conflict.

In Islamic belief, God cannot have a son. It is an insult to him to say such a thing. In Islamic belief, God is so transcendent he could never take the form of mankind as Jesus did. In Islamic belief, Jesus did not die on the cross. There is no need for substitutionary death anyway, since serving Allah faithfully will guarantee a place in heaven. So, in their doctrine, Jesus can only be a minor prophet. So this is the point of conflict: the identity of Jesus. Who do we say he is? Do we honor him? Do we insist on proper reverence to his name? Do we take issue with those who use his name as a curse word? I don't want anyone to be neutral about Jesus. And they won't be if you proclaim him as God. You will start conflict. Maybe even a riot. But you will also start someone to thinking. "Whom do I say that Jesus is?

In the final analysis, however, it is what we do that convinces people. Is your lifestyle and conduct a verification of your claim that Jesus is Lord? Do others see you make key decisions based on the Lordship of Jesus in your life? Many of you have just made a decision to attend a Bible college. You are serious about answering your call, and you want to get trained. You are making some sacrifices to do so. As you continue to follow his call, your credibility as a witness will increase. Let me encourage you to see it through on a day-by-day basis. May you be a living witness to all who know you that Jesus is Lord of your life!

SAVING CAPTAIN FUCHIDA

"Ye have heard that it hath been said, Thou shalt love thy neighbour, and hate thine enemy. But I say unto you, Love your enemies, bless them that curse you, do good to them that hate you, and pray for them which despitefully use you, and persecute you;" Matthew 5:43-44

"There are some people who have inflicted such horrible evil upon you that you know you will never forgive them. Imagine what you will say if you meet them in Heaven!"

Let me tell you about a time when I shook the hand of a man who led the most vicious attack on America in recorded history before the terrorist attacks in September, 2001. Jesus can forgive anybody, even someone like me. Yet in my natural self, I am prone to think that certain evil men in this world can only enter Eternity in the fires of Hell. That is what, in my natural mind, I would say concerning those men who perpetrated the unspeakable atrocity of the attack on our country September 11, 2001. Yet I have personally met a man just like that; a man whom God had forgiven and saved. I was a student attending New Orleans Baptist Theological Seminary in 1967 when a chapel speaker was introduced as the man who led the Japanese air strike on Pearl Harbor. His name was Mitsuo Fuchida. He became a Christian after the war and started serving the Lord as an international evangelist. At first, I couldn't believe I was hearing right when he was introduced.

Some background would help at this point. As a young boy, I listened daily to the radio news about the war. I heard about the atrocities the Japanese had committed. I knew what a horrible evil the attack on Pearl Harbor was. Killed in that one day were 3,077 sailors and 226 soldiers. Another 1200 were wounded. Eight battleships were turned into raging infernos of horror and agony and death. Hatred of Japanese people was seared into the hearts of all Americans on December 7, 1941 on the day President Roosevelt said would "live in infamy." During the war, I heard the remarks of adults. I knew that Americans hated "Japs," as they called them. During the war, hatred grew as we heard about the Bataan Death March and treatment of American prisoners in the concentration camps. In my home community there were families who lost fathers or brothers or sons in the war against Japan. Children even played games about killing Japs. I grew up hating the Japanese.

Now, in a seminary chapel service, I was hearing a Jap talk to me about Christ. Not just any Jap, but the very one who led the infamous attack at Pearl. This was the commander who ordered the huge flight of 360 attack planes to dive on our ships and barracks and start bombing, yelling into their radios the war cry, "Tora, Tora, Tora!" You cannot imagine the emotions I found myself trying to sort out. I knew I should I love him now as a Christian brother – like the early Christian community learned to love Saul, the former mad killer of Christians. But how could I? As I listened to his story, my heart gradually warmed.

After the war, Fuchida went home a defeated warrior and became a farmer to support his family. In 1950 he received a tract written by Jacob DeShazer as he stepped off a train in Tokyo. The title of the tract caught his attention: "I was a Prisoner of Japan." DeShazer, one of the famous Doolittle Raiders, trusted Christ while held prisoner in a Japanese concentration camp for 40 months. He later went to Japan as a missionary and preached Christ to the nation who held him captive. Fuchida was so stirred by this testimony that he received Christ himself and faithfully served the Lord until his death in 1976.

I knew Christ had forgiven Fuchida, and now I must. I was in seminary training to be a man of God. How could I go forward in the ministry unless I let Jesus wash the hatred out of my heart. At the close of that chapel service, I was one of the students who shook the hand of the man who bombed Pearl Harbor. I remember the momentary meeting of our eyes. In that moment, I can truthfully say that I no longer held any hatred for him, or for the Japanese people.

Today we live under the evil cloud of terrorism. The attacks using passenger planes as bombs on September 11, 2001 and subsequent beheadings of innocent civilians or suicide bombings have brought a level of hatred to our hearts. Islamic fundamentalists in particular and Islamic people in general, are harder to love now than ever before. And how would you feel if the Al Quaida leader who plotted the attacks of September 11 became converted to Christ and gave a testimony in your church?

In a lesser way, all of us are tested almost daily. We all have scars of wounds inflicted upon us by others around us. We have been hurt so badly, we feel we can never forgive these people. Yet that is exactly what our Lord says we have to do. We must not only forgive them, but love them enough to pray God's blessings upon them. That kind of love is only available if Christ lives in your heart. Let Him in, and He will help you love your enemies. Hate your enemies and you will shut Him out. It's time to let the Lord heal our wounds, so that we can go on to enjoy the blessings of God in our life.

TO WHOM WILL YOU GIVE YOUR GIFTS?

"And when they were come into the house, they saw the young child with Mary his mother, and fell down, and worshipped him: and when they had opened their treasures, they presented unto him gifts; gold and frankincense, and myrrh." Matthew 2:11

"Who will get your inheritance? You do have one, and you will give it away. That's not the question. Through life and legacy, you will give away your entire inheritance. But who gets it? That's the question."

This is the well-read and much-loved story of the wise men that came to worship Jesus just after the Incarnation. They announced their first objective in Matthew 2:2, "...Where is he...?" That was the first objective for all of us. Finding Jesus. As Satan's representative in this story, Herod did not want the wise men to find Jesus. He still doesn't want people to find Jesus. But God ordains that all men may! The wise men did find Jesus, as all wise men still do. And when they found him, they worshiped him. They had treasures with them, and they opened them and gave them to Jesus. The three things mentioned are highly significant. There was gold, signifying sovereignty. Frankincense, signifying death. Myrrh, signifying suffering.

The treasures were their own, but they gave them all to

Jesus. These represent the most valuable things you have to give away. You already have what the gold represents. You are a king, because God gave you sovereign right over your own soul. You have sovereignty over your own choices! But you will give it away. You will either give it to Satan or to Christ, but you cannot keep it. The myrrh also represents something you own. It's suffering or just plain trouble. You are born for trouble. In the world you will have it. Jesus said so.

Your trouble is personal. Nobody in this world has been inside your skin and known exactly what you have gone through – except you. But it has shaped the person you have become. In a larger sense, myrrh stands for your whole life struggle. Does it have any meaning? Yes. Every life has meaning. And one of the greatest needs we have is to believe that our life on earth makes a difference. We need to know our struggle is significant. But you will have to turn it over to someone: either Jesus or the Devil. Nobody lives neutrally.

The other gift was frankincense. That too represents something you have. It represents your death. Most people don't want to take ownership of their personal death. In fact, they don't want to even think about it. Yet mankind always views as heroes those who make the ultimate sacrifice for some noble cause. It is actually the most valuable thing we have! You had no control over your birth, but your death is entirely different. You were not born as a Christian, but you can die as one.

You can take this treasure and use it to die as a nobody, a

loser, or even as a villain. Or you can give your death to Jesus and die as somebody in the Kingdom of God , a real winner, and a hero to others. So the question is an extremely personal one: to whom will you give your gifts? After meeting Jesus, you should give your crown to him: let him rule in your life. You should give the myrrh of your life struggle to him, let it be a witness to him. You should give your ultimate accomplishment, your own death, to him. We note in verse 12, that the wise men did not go back through Jerusalem and meet with the crafty old King Herod. After they met Jesus, they went another way. They chose another path. They chose not to go back the way they came. Once you have opened your treasures and given them all to Jesus, you will take a different path.

JESUS IS MOVING; DON'T LET HIM PASS BY

"And they told him, that Jesus of Nazareth passeth by." Luke 18:37

"There are moments in your life when your entire future depends on calling out to Jesus for help. You cannot waste a second more. You have to call on Him then; or He will pass on by."

That was the case with blind Bartimaeus of Jericho. As he sat by the wayside begging, something unusual began to happen. He heard a multitude of people moving his way. Jesus was about to pass by. This was his one opportunity. If he had not called out to Jesus at that moment, he would regret it the rest of his days. The same moment of opportunity was offered to the two disciples on the road to Emmaus after the crucifixion. As Cleopas and his wife Mary reflected upon the events of the last week, Jesus joined them, but they could not recognize Him. They talked all the way to a spot in the road in front of their home. Jesus made as if he would go on further (Luke 24:28). But they constrained him to go home with them. There was a moment like that on a dark night in the Sea of Galilee. The disciples were amazed to see Jesus walking on the water, and He would have passed by them (Mark 6:48). But they cried out to Him, and He came into the boat with them. Zaccheus in Jericho had such a moment. He knew Jesus was to pass by a certain place, and he ran ahead and climbed a tree so that he could see Jesus better. People got in his way at first, but he quickly got past that problem and found a solution. It was good that he did so, because when Jesus got there, He looked up and invited Himself to the home of Zaccheus that very day.

One recent Sunday morning while attending a Sunday School class at West Metro Church of God, my mind drifted a bit and I found myself meditating upon how Jesus moves quickly through our life at special seasons. We know it is a genuine presence of Jesus, but unless we make some kind of response, He will go on by. Then my mind moved to the words of the hymn by Fanny Crosby: "Pass Me Not." I remembered that when I was a teen, I heard that song for the first time in a revival service. It was at old Brooklyn Church, just up the road from our farm in north Lousiana. I remembered that it was the first hymn that strangely stirred my heart to hunger to be saved. This was going through my mind as the Sunday School class ended. Then during worship only a few minutes later, to my amazement the choir began to sing "Pass Me Not." I realized God was impressing a message on me. It was not so much a message to preach, but a lesson to be learned. And that is why I am sharing this with you. The hymn to which I refer was written by Fanny Crosby in the 1870's. Blinded by an improper medication when she was a baby, Fanny lived a remarkable and productive life, writing over 8,000 hymns. This song is especially significant, because it was inspired by a Bible character who was also blind – Bartimaeus.

Listen to the words of the first line that she wrote: "Pass me not, O gentle Savior, Hear my humble cry; While on others Thou art calling, Do not pass me by. "Saviour, Savior, Hear my humble cry; While on others Thou art calling, Do not pass me by." Can you feel the pathos of such a person who sits in permanent darkness and helplessness, crying out to Jesus? Can you hear the urgency in the uplifted tone, crying, "Savior, Savior?" I know that the Lord showed me through that song that this is what you and I must do in those special, life-defining moments. We must get into a mode of desperation that brings an earnest, urgent prayer for help.

You may be going through some storm right now. But somewhere in that storm, Jesus is walking toward you on the water. Invite Him into your boat. It could be that you are pondering questions about Jesus. Invite Him into your home like the two on the road to Emmaus. You may be praying for a great need to be met. You may be calling out to Him like Bartimaeus, but need to cry louder. Like Zaccheus, you may need a better look at Jesus and you may have to just look over the heads of people around you. Others may get in your way, but if you try hard enough, you will see Jesus. But keep in mind Jesus is moving. If you show no interest in the help that only He can give, He will pass you by. Call out now before this moment slips away.

WITHOUT HIM

"All things were made by him; and without him was not any thing made that was made." "For by him were all things created, that are in heaven, and that are in earth, visible and invisible, whether they be thrones, or dominions, or principalities, or powers: all things were created by him, and for him: And he is before all things, and by him all things consist." "I am the vine, ye are the branches: He that abideth in me, and I in him, the same bringeth forth much fruit: for without me ye can do nothing." John 1:3; Col. 1:16, 17; John 15:5

"Real things of real and lasting value are not made by man and cannot be sustained by man."

In July of 1969, I stood in the lobby of an Arab hotel in East

Jerusalem watching the television news, seeing a United States astronaut stepping out of the lunar landing module onto the surface of the moon. We heard Neil Armstrong say, "That's one small step for a man; one giant leap for mankind." Cheers went up from the crowd in the lobby, and one man grabbed me and kissed me on both cheeks, and exclaimed, "You Americans are wonderful. You can do anything!" Of course those Arabs in that hotel lobby and the whole world know now that we cannot do "anything" we wish to do. We can only do the things God permits, and only do it with material he has provided, and only do it by physical laws he has set up. One day a Christian physicist was debating two atheistic scientists. He told them God created man from the dust of the earth. They said, "Science can do that. Bring some dirt and we'll show you." The Christian said, "No way. You have to invent your own dirt out of nothing."

There is a strong statement here for ministry. If you accomplish anything of real and lasting value, you must do it with God. Your ministry can only be participatory. Without him not any thing was or can be made. Jesus said, "Without me, you can do nothing!" Without the vine, the branches cannot produce any fruit at all. Even in your relationship with Jesus, you must wait for your season. Your fruit will not remain if it is attempted too early or too late. How self-confident are we about our own know-how? Have we ever thought that it was some other factor that was missing? Have you caught yourself saying, "If I just had the money I know I could make it big?" Have we ever thought it was someone else holding us back?

But if you don't have a right relationship with Jesus, it's not money you need. It's not having someone get out of your way. It's you that can't do anything that works.

I challenge you to go back to acknowledging the one who made the world; the one who holds it all together. He can do anything, and you can't do anything. He that called you is also ready to do it. You will become the glove, and he will be the hand inside you making it happen. But it's his holy hand that will get the glory. If the glove starts wanting its own glory, he can very easily lay it aside. Let's pray today for a new sense of absolute dependence upon his power working in us.

UBI CHRISTUS

"In whom all the building fitly framed together groweth unto an holy temple in the Lord: In whom ye also are builded together for an habitation of God through the Spirit." Ephesians 2:21-22

"Don't try to carry Christ with you wherever you go. How big to you think you are? Rather, let Him carry you wherever He wants to go."

Jesus is building the real Church in this world. We are becoming corporately a single world-wide entity: His living temple. We are built together in Christ to be a habitation of God through the Spirit. The key principle of ecclesiology is that Christ is building His Church. This idea helps us understand the true nature of the Church. It exists only where He is. There is a Latin phrase which expresses this theological concept. It is "Ubi Christus, ibi Ecclesia." It means, "Where Christ is, there is the Church." Therefore, a Church ceases to exist where Christ is not at work. Where Christ is at work, that is where you will find the true Church. This simple key may help us understand the confusion of so many conflicting models of "church" that we find in modern Christendom.

We love to speak of ecumenicity and diversity and inclusiveness. Yet some of these church models are so far from the New Testament norms that they really do not seem to be churches at all. Some models declare messages that conflict the messages of other models. They cannot all be expressions of the true Church. Only to the extent that they are doing what Christ is doing are they part of the true Church. And what is He doing? He is there among the poor in the slums and favelas. He is there with the homeless refugees from war-torn areas. He is there with the hungry victims of famine. He is with the AIDS orphans. He is there with His persecuted Church. He is there with the missionaries who are taking the gospel to the unreached peoples of the world. Here is the secret to having a true New Testament church: find where Jesus is working, and do it with Him. There you will find the sweetness of His presence, and enjoy the fellowship of His Church. There you will find the anointing for which you have hungered so long. How can you find where Jesus is moving right now? You get your clues from what He did in the New Testament. With which kinds of people were you most likely to find Him then? He is still the same Jesus. Look among the same kinds of groups, and there He is!

Do you really hunger to be in the center of God's will? Then look around and see where Jesus is working today. "Ubi Christus, ibi Ecclesia." Be a part of the action, and you will find your place in the true Church. By the Spirit you will be "fitly framed" into your place in the Church. Your life will fall into place. But don't seek a title first. Find your function first. Your spiritual gifts and your recognized office will follow your function. Pray for eyes to see true movements of Christ in this world. Identify so fully with Jesus that wherever He is working, you will make yourself available. That is where your calling will take you.

WHAT WILL BECOME OF ALL YOUR ACHIEVEMENTS?

"Every man's work shall be made manifest: for the day shall declare it, because it shall be revealed by fire; and the fire shall try every man's work of what sort it is. If any man's work abide which he hath built thereupon, he shall receive a reward. If any man's work shall be burned, he shall suffer loss: but he himself shall be saved; yet so as by fire." I Corinthians 3:13-15

"Time and eternity place their own value on our so-called achievements. How much will be left 50 years from now, or 200 years from now?"

Moses in Psalm 90 asks God to teach us to number our days – that we may apply our hearts to wisdom. God mightily used him as a great lawgiver and teacher. Though he has been gone over 3,400 years, he continues to influence civilization. As you come to classes here I want to challenge you to learn the priority of the eternal. As early as possible, get a glimpse of the timeless perspective of God on the things of your life.

In 1969 I participated in the first season of a five-year archaeological excavation at Beersheba, Israel. As we removed each shovel-full of dirt, we carefully sifted it through a wire mesh. It was instructive to me to notice what few items still remained of the lives that had been lived in that place. Sometimes we found a metal trinket – something once among the valuables treasured by a noble family. Other times we found a serving bowl that had once been part of a kitchen. Or it might be one small coin that had in a previous century been part of a vast hoard of wealth. Not much else. Only fragments of names here and there. No personal histories at all. Only a few small relics left of nameless lives that have faded into oblivion. I think about my house, furniture, book collection, clothes, bank account, and car. Obviously, in the scales of eternity their worth will quickly diminish to nothing. Normally, I don't even think about how much such "stuff" I have. Then when my family moves from one house to another, I realize I have way too much clutter.

I want to make sure that what I leave behind when I exit this life is more than this clutter that will wind up in some thrift store or yard sale. What I accomplish in this life must transcend material things. I must impact society in some positive way. I must influence eternal souls. I must leave a godly heritage among my children and future descendants. I must be laying up some treasure in heaven. It is good that I give some attention now to putting more time and energy on heavenly priorities. In I Corinthians 3, the Word of God tells us that every man's work will be tried. Worthless works will be burned up. But why should I wait until then to at least think about how I am spending my time? It would be wise to spend the greatest amount of our allotted time on things with an eternal value. It may be that God is calling you today to give up some trivial pursuit that will just eat up your time. It may be that God is calling upon you today to spend more time on something that will last for time and eternity. In the words of Ecclesiastes 3:6, this is "a time to get, and a time to lose; a time to keep, and a time to cast away;"

DAILY MIRACLES OF PROVISION AT SULFUR SPRINGS

"Wherefore, if God so clothe the grass of the field, which to day is, and to morrow is cast into the oven, shall he not much more clothe you, O ye of little faith? Therefore take no thought, saying What shall we eat? Or, What shall we drink? Or, Wherewithal shall we be clothed? (For after all these things do the Gentiles seek:) for your heavenly Father knoweth that ye have need of all these things. But seek ye first the kingdom of God, and his righteousness; and all these things shall be added unto you. Take therefore no thought for the morrow: for the morrow shall take thought for the things of itself. Sufficient unto the day is the evil thereof." Matthew 6:30-34

"Our heavenly Father daily loads us down with benefits. Sometimes we are given seasons of life in which we learn to appreciate our daily load of benefits."

When I was a brand-new Christian, just released from jail in New Orleans, I was homeless. I walked the streets daily with my head down, looking for loose change on the sidewalk. When I had picked up about 65 cents, I had enough for a meal at Royal Castle. Even today I bend over to pick up a penny. I learned how important it was to appreciate every little provision. When we were newly married in 1959, we moved to a rural church parsonage in North Mississippi. My salary then was $50 a week, most of which went on car payments, furniture payments and gas for the car. We had no insurance at all. We didn't have enough for groceries or medicine. At times we ate just a single baked potato for supper. Often I will kill a squirrel or quail and we would have it for breakfast. But we never went without a single meal. There were many times we found a small bag of groceries on the front steps. Sometimes we would find a few potatoes or peanuts. At other times we found fresh roasting ears of corn someone had left for us. Frequently we made a meal of a single item: peanuts for supper and potatoes for breakfast.

In the next year, our first child was born, our daughter Teresa. I knew I wouldn't have the cost of the hospital charges. So I tried selling the first fresh peaches of the season off the back of a borrowed pickup. I broke the axle of the pickup and all the earnings went for repairs. I tried raising a patch of watermelons. The night before the watermelons were to be harvested and trucked out, a herd of dairy cattle destroyed the whole patch. I cried and prayed, and the Lord told me he would provide. So sure enough, when my wife and baby were released, we had paid some on the bill and settled on a repayment plan. It was soon paid for. We needed a special formula for the baby. I would go to a little crossroads store and put things on account. When the account grew to more than I could pay back, I cried and prayed again. Again the Lord reminded me that he would provide. On the next trip to the store, I found that someone had paid my account in full. I was learning great things about the faithfulness of God!

God kept providing. During those two years I served in that place, God proved that he could daily supply all our needs. I learned an important lesson. Serve the Lord and put him first. Then all these things that we normally worry about will be just added back into our lives – as regular as clockwork. Psalms 68:19 says that our Lord daily loads us with benefits. God routinely, daily loads us with benefits such as food, clothing, shelter, money, health, freedom, and much, much more. Have you stopped to thank him for your benefits today? Those who would be ministers must first learn how to be grateful to God. I often encounter ministers with an attitude of ingratitude. Their people can never do enough for them. They always want a "bigger package." But the best package I can recommend to you is the one I discovered in those early years. It is the package of faith in God. Just depend upon God and do everything you can to pay your bills in an honest way. Make sure that the very first bill you pay is your tithe. After that, just wait and see what God will do!

RESTORING A '63 EL CAMINO IS HARD WORK

"BRETHREN, if a man be overtaken in a fault, ye which are spiritual, restore such an one in the spirit of meekness, considering thyself, lest thou also be tempted." Galatians 6:1

"To restore something that is broken is hard work. We are tempted to toss it aside. We live in a disposable age: not only do we manufacture disposable things, but we often find it easier to dispose of things that are broken than to repair them. However, we must never treat human beings as disposable."

In the mid-eighties, while I was out of a job and suffering from Lupus, a kind Christian brother, Joel Hammond, gave me an old El Camino truck. Its bed was rusted out, and it had no motor. But my friend also gave me a used 6-cylinder motor that would fit it. He towed it to my farm and told me when I felt better I might want to restore it and sell it for a little income. Even though I continued to suffer from joint pain, I took advantage of occasional "good days" to work on the truck. Little by little I replaced the rusted parts and then rigged a beam between two pine trees. My wife Jackie and I then hoisted the motor and rolled the truck in place under it. We lowered the motor and attached the clutch to the transmission. Then we bolted the motor to the motor mounts on the frame. We carefully reattached all the wires, carburetor levers, gas line and hoses. Then with a new battery, oil in the crankcase, and gas in the tank, we started it up on the first try! But we were nowhere near through with the work. Day by day as my illness permitted, I sanded away the rough spots in the paint. We drove it to Maaco and got it a new coat of paint. Then came new tires and hub caps. Finally, weeks of hard work after we began, we had a restored El Camino – as good as it looked when it came from the factory.

I drove it on several ministry trips before we sold it. But that was one of the hardest projects my wife and I ever had. There were so many times we found another broken part or tried to budge a rusty bolt and we thought, "Let's quit now. Let's just tow it to the junkyard. We'll never get it restored. What were we thinking?" But we couldn't give up and despise something our brother gave us to help us. Today, people are tempted to think like that about their broken marriages, or about troublesome children, or about some disgraceful church member. Just walk away and get a new marriage. Or just shut them out of your life. Disposable relationships! God help us.

We had the essential parts for that El Camino. We had the body and the chassis and the motor. They just weren't in the right order. Some hard work was required, but it was worth the effort. Even more so, it takes sometimes takes persistence and hard work to put a wrecked human being back together. The essential parts are still there. There just needs to be a reassembly of things in the right order. Yet there is no more rewarding restoration project. Besides, if we obey the Lord we don't have any option but to try. In a way, we're all "fix-up" projects. Praise God that He didn't give up on any of us! Take a moment to reflect on how God has used people in your life to "restore" you!

SOUNDS OF SILENCE

"And when he had sent the multitudes away, he went up into a mountain apart to pray: and when the evening was come, he was there alone." Matthew 14:23

"When you are quiet in a solitary place you hear new sounds: crickets, birds, and the still small voice of the Spirit."

Jesus took the time to go to a quiet place to be alone with the Father. He's our role model. It is extremely unwise to spend all your time with noise. We were designed by God to need quiet times for our spiritual nature. We need times to hear in the spirit. But our flesh nature wants to drown out all such input. That's why we seem frightened by the sounds of silence. If the house is too quiet, we turn on a radio or television. When we are visiting with a friend, we fill up all the moments of time with speaking. We get uncomfortable if we allow a lull in the conversation.

I recall three pivotal periods in my life when silence provided necessary atmosphere for the Holy Spirit to lead me into life-changing decisions. The first period was forced on me in a jail, but led to my salvation experience with Christ. As an 18-year old, the confinement was the worst and best thing that ever happened to me. I thought at the time that it was the worst, but now think it was the best. The second pivotal period of silence was voluntary, and led to a fullness of the Holy Spirit that I had never known before. I reached a desperation level in my life and found my self in a search mode – a quest for more of the power of God in my life. I was alone on a plane, late at night when God gave me the wonderful visitation I was seeking. The third greatly significant time of silence led to my answering the call of God to be a full-time teacher of the Word of God. I was dying of Lupus and confined to a hospital bed, alone in another state. There in that solitude God spoke to me and healed me and gave me the calling I walk in now. Of course there have been hundreds of other periods of more-than-usual quietness. Those have led to fresh direction or deeper spiritual insight or answered prayers.

Think about it. You have been cheated. How much quality quiet time just happens in a normal day for you? The world, the flesh, and the devil have conspired against you, to keep you away from quietness. Part of you hungers for quietness, and part of you hates it! But now you can do as Jesus did and make an intentional rearrangement. He sent the crowds away.

He went aside into a solitary place. Why should you feel threatened by silence? Why should you equate quietness with loneliness? Why should you feel quiet times are a waste of time? Are these not blatant lies of the Devil? Reject these feelings and make room for silence!

Quietness provides the best setting for some spiritual disciplines that too few Christians today experience. Among these are spiritual listening, meditation, and private devotions, Bible study, and prayer. When you are quiet in a solitary place, you will begin to hear new sounds: the breeze in trees, crickets chirping, birds singing and your own heartbeat. Most important of all: you will be able to hear the still small voice of the Spirit of God. Why not determine right now that you will find a quiet place and a quiet time for daily listening?

WHEN SOMEONE MISTREATS YOU, IT'S A TEST

"But I say unto you which hear, Love your enemies, do good to them which hate you, Bless them that curse you, and pray for them which despitefully use you." Luke 6:27-28

"God sometimes allows us to be tested by the mistreatment of others. The tests challenge us at our weakest points so that those areas can be strengthened in the character of Christ."

In the early seventies my family and I were planting a new church in Decatur, Georgia. On Sundays the congregation of

Our Shepherd's Church met at Snapfinger Elementary School, but during the week our various small groups met in homes. God gave us a great breakthrough in reaching youth in the drug culture, and something had to be done to disciple them as quickly as possible. Newly converted hippies started meeting with me for Bible study on Monday nights in our home on Lee Street. These new Christians brought van-loads of dirty, smelly, shaggy-haired friends to hear the message of Christ. They would pick them up from the streets and from hang-out spots along the Chattahoochee River. All of them reeked of marijuana. But excitement stirred more excitement, as well as curiosity, and they came. God mightily blessed, and soon our living room had overflowed. We held our Bible studies most of the summer of 1973 on the front lawn of our home. Our neighbors soon became accustomed to seeing 40 or 40 youth sitting cross-legged on the lawn with their Bibles open.

Some of the young people had taken to drugs because they were from dysfunctional homes, and they were struggling with a good deal of emotional baggage concerning parents and authority figures. One Sunday night my family and I returned home to find graffiti sprayed in paint all over our house. That house was the first place we had owned, and we had taken considerable pains to keep it neat and attractive. The exterior was dark brown brick, and we had freshly painted all the door casing and window trim in a complimentary shade of rose. We had just installed new aluminum window screens. All the shrubs had been neatly trimmed. We had made it picture-perfect, and now someone had defaced everything! As we arrived that Sunday night to find dark splotches of green paint sprayed on the new window screens, on the brick, and on the carefully painted trim work, we were numb with shock. We got out of the car and just stood on the sidewalk for a moment in silence, but then somehow I realized that this was a test. I had just been teaching on forgiveness and loving your enemies enough to pray for them. My wife Jackie realized that it was a test about the same moment. We joined hands with our children Teresa and Douglas and began to pray aloud.

First of all, we prayed that God would forgive the person who had done this. Then we said in the prayer that we ourselves forgave the person who had trashed us. We thanked God for the house He had given us, and we thanked God for the happiness we had in our home. We prayed that whoever had done this to us would soon feel the happiness we enjoyed. On the next Wednesday night, a teenage girl who had been attending our Monday night home meetings confessed that she had trashed our house. Moreover, she had been hiding behind the shrubbery and heard the prayer we prayed. She was waiting to see us explode with anger, and when she heard us praying for God to forgive her, it was more than she could stand. She gave her heart to the Lord.

How we thanked God that by His grace we had been able to pass that test! And how that lesson stayed with us over the years! Jesus taught us to love our enemies and pray for them that despitefully use us. In our spiritual development, every lesson will be followed by a test. That's only natural. The purpose of a test is to show you where your strengths and weaknesses are. Is someone mistreating you? It's a test of your forgiveness. Be careful how you react. Someone may be watching to see how you handle it. Can you do what Jesus taught you to do? Remember, that you are forgiven as you forgive others. Pray for the ones who mistreat you, and let God do the rest!

YOU MUST LEAVE SOMETHING BEHIND TO GET WHAT YOU'RE MISSING

"And Jesus, walking by the sea of Galilee, saw two brethren, Simon called Peter, and Andrew his brother, casting a net into the sea: for they were fishers. And he saith unto them, Follow me, and I will make you fishers of men. And they straightway left their nets, and followed him. And going on from thence, he saw other two brethren, James the son of Zebedee, and John his brother, in a ship with Zebedee their father, mending their nets; and he called them. And they immediately left the ship and their father, and followed him." Matthew 4:18-22

"It is a spiritual law that in order to find what's missing in your life you must leave something behind."

To follow Jesus means that you will leave something behind. You will leave behind a so-called comfort zone. When you look back, you will wonder why you ever thought that lifestyle was comfortable! You will leave behind a sense of loss and lack of significance. You find yourself fulfilled only in the pursuit of what you were designed for and born for! To follow Jesus means most of all that you won't die a meaningless death at the end of a meaningless life and go an eternal hell and suffer forever as a meaningless soul. Your soul was created by God on purpose at the moment of conception. He has a plan for you. He designed you to accomplish something significant in his kingdom. But if you die without following Jesus, you waste an eternal soul!

In the case of these two brothers, they left behind a secure income. They were professionals: they had a ship and nets and an established market for their fish. They even had nets in the water. But the text says that they immediately left their nets and followed Jesus. A little farther along Jesus called two more brothers who were in the same business, but they didn't have any nets in the water at the time. They were just mending their nets, planning on a better future. But when Jesus called them, they left the ship and nets with their father, and immediately they followed Jesus!

The word, "follow," used here is the Greek word *akoloutheo* which means "to be in the same pathway with." You can't follow Jesus and stay where you are. He's moving. He's going up a different pathway than yours. To follow, you have to change pathways. Besides that, you can't follow so far behind you lose sight of Jesus. You must be where He is on the pathway. Note also that the whole focus of your life must change.

You will no longer focus on fishing or making a living. You will focus on people. You will become a fisher of men, bringing others into relationship with Jesus. There's nothing in this world more satisfying! It's what you were designed for.

Following Jesus also means traveling without excess baggage. In his earthly ministry he traveled light. When he sent out the disciples on missions he told them to travel light – take not even an extra coat or sandals. For some who wanted to follow him, he warned them that "...foxes have holes and the birds of the air have nests, but the Son of Man has nowhere to lay his head" (Luke 9:58). There was no guarantee that he would put them up in nice hotels. For many of us, our lifestyle has become our excess baggage. We are called upon to be ready to leave it if it hinders us.

Years ago I realized that I had a choice. I could be like Demas who forsook Paul in the Roman prison, "...having loved this present world..." (II Timothy 4:10). Or I could be like the disciples who forsook all and followed him. I made a conscious decision to live a simpler life. I moved my family out of a nice suburban home to a mobile home in the country. We stopped eating in fancy restaurants. We started shopping for clothes at K-mart or Walmart, or even at thrift stores. I scaled down from fancy lease cars to dependable but affordable transportation. That's when I began to make overseas mission trips at my own expense.

My family and I found something we were missing. When we gave up things for the ministry, God gave back into our lives - a richness and quality we had never known before. It shaped a godly character in our children that they in turn are shaping in our grandchildren. And we enjoyed more adventures than ever before. Near home we fished, backpacked, went on picnics. God even provided vacation trips to Florida, or even Cape Cod. Once we took a van, and camping at KOA's along the way, made a tour of historic sites from Williamsburg to Philadelphia. Each member of the family at times would travel with me to Europe, the Middle East, or Central America. We never regretted giving up things to follow Jesus. Jesus makes you the same offer today: "Follow me, and I will make you fishers of men."

TWO SEAS

"In the last day, that great day of the feast, Jesus stood and cried, saying, If any man thirst, let him come unto me, and drink. He that believeth on me, as the scripture hath said, out of his belly shall flow rivers of living water. (But this spake he of the Spirit, which they that believe on him should receive: for the Holy Ghost was not yet given; because that Jesus was not yet glorified.)" John 7: 37-39

"Selfish and Christian are two adjectives that cannot be used together. Christian nature opposes selfishness."

Jesus wants to so abundantly supply us with His Spirit that rivers of blessing will flow from us into other lives. He used the picture of rivers – things that flow from abundance. When we are filled with His Spirit, we cannot help but impart good things to other people around us. Selfishness does not fit into that kind of life. The more Christian you are, the more you will have a giving nature. "Freely you have received; freely give" (Matthew 10:8).

I can't tell you how much my familiarity with the land of the Bible has enriched me. I began to travel frequently to Israel and surrounding countries in 1969. Space here does not permit me to share all the revelations and insights that came when I was actually on one of the sites of the biblical stories. But let me share an insight gained concerning some symbolism about the Holy Spirit. There are two tiny seas in the land of the Bible. You have heard so much of each of them that they are probably much bigger in your mind than they actually are. The Sea of Galilee is really a fresh water lake. It is about 7 miles wide and thirteen miles long. The Dead Sea is a salt water basin less than 7 miles wide and thirty miles long. During more than 30 Holy Land tours, I have often been in the waters of both.

These two lakes are so different that they often are used as examples of contrast. There are only two things that they have in common. One is that they are both located in the Great Rift Valley that runs through the Middle East on a north-south axis. The second is that they are both fed by the Jordan River. In almost every other way, they are entirely different. The Sea of Galilee is full of fish and supports lush agriculture around it through irrigation. Its waters supply the population of many cities throughout Israel. The Dead Sea is empty of life and the land around it is barren. Its waters are poisonous.

What makes the difference? In the case of the Sea of Galilee, water flows in and water flows out. But no waters flow out of the Dead Sea. It only takes. It never gives. The Dead Sea is located so far below sea level that no rivers can run out of it. So it accumulates all the mineral sediments from the waters of the Jordan, the Zered and the Arnon Rivers. And over the centuries the amount of the minerals gradually choked the life out of the Dead Sea. When I first began to visit it in the late sixties, the sea was only one-fourth solid. In 2004, it was already one-third solid. It is so buoyant that you cannot sink in it. To sit and float in it feels much like sitting in a water-filled mattress. But its water is slimy to touch, and irritates the skin. It must be washed off immediately.

We all know people who are like that. You have to "wash off" their effect on you. Otherwise, you too will become negative, suspicious and selfish. Those people are always taking from you and others. But they never give. There is a powerful lesson here for all of us. Take a spiritual inventory: which sea best represents the way you live? Paul reminds us that Jesus said, "It is more blessed to give than to receive" (Acts 20:35). That means that there is a higher dimension of life that we can have if we give more than we receive. That seems impossible to the natural mind, but it is absolutely possible for those who spiritually come to Jesus for "living water." You can give and keep on giving; and you'll never run dry!

A TRUE STORY

"And there were in the same country shepherds abiding in the field, keeping watch over their flock by night. And, lo, the angel of the Lord came upon them, and the glory of the Lord shone round about them; and they were sore afraid. And the angel said unto them, Fear not: for behold, I bring you good tidings of great joy, which shall be to all people. For unto you is born this day in the city of David a Saviour, which is Christ the Lord. And this shall be a sign unto you; Ye shall find the babe wrapped in swaddling clothes, lying in a manger. And suddenly there was with the angel a multitude of the heavenly host praising God, and saying, Glory to God in the highest, and on earth peace, good will toward men." Luke 2:8-14

"Earliest childhood recollections of Christmas often leave in our minds a Christmas story not too different than that of the Easter bunny and the tooth fairy – it's just not real to us. And some theologians haven't changed that for us."

Think back to your earliest impressions of Christmas. Most of you knew it was special, but you didn't know why. You thought you did – because you believed what you were told. I was no different. I grew up in spartan conditions in the post Depression era on a farm. There was no running water and no electricity. Of course our Christmas decorations had to be very different than those we have now. My mom used to take three small children on a short walk through the snow out into the woods, where we would select the best little holly tree we could find – one that was filled with red berries. She would encourage me on as I, the oldest child at about 6 or 7 years of age, would work valiantly at the job of cutting down the tiny tree. We would take it home, stand it up in a bucket of soil, and begin to decorate it. Small containers of gold or silver paint were poured over the top of buckets of water. The paint would float in a thin layer, and we would dip sweetgum balls into it to make gold and silver balls to put on the tree. Soon we had a glorious tree, with a silver star covered with foil from salvaged gum wrappers crowning the very top.

For Christmas Day, Mom would use her limited resources to put together a delicious cake – usually a coconut-raisin layer cake – with real eggs and freshly grated coconut. And on Christmas morning, there would be at least one small toy under the tree for each of us. They weren't wrapped – we just knew which toy was for whom. And there would be a sock stuffed with fresh fruit and nuts - a rarity in mid-winter. So we all knew Christmas was something special. Christmas Eve was the night Santa would visit our home – if we had been good. But it would be years before I would hear the true story.

When I finally did, I was a young man with an angry and rebellious nature, constantly in trouble with the law. I was saved in a New Orleans jail while reading the good news of John 3:16. As a young Christian I began to understand the true story of Christmas. I was called to preach when I was saved, and as soon as I got out on parole, I started pastoring small churches. Frequently, just before Christmas, we would get phone calls from members who wanted to read the Christmas story to their children, but they didn't know where in the Bible to find it.

By the time I had been a Christian a few years, I had grown in the Lord and I was in love with the Word of God and had read every word of it – several times. I couldn't imagine church members who had been Christians for years knowing so little of the Christmas story that they did not even know where to find it in the Bible! Yet as I went on to study at various colleges and seminaries over the years, I found that the Christmas story was not very real even to some theologians! They would discuss the awesome "Hupostasis" in dry and analytical lectures. Hupostasis is the theological term for the mysterious union of two natures in the person of Christ: divine and human.

In the Incarnation, the Son of God forever changed the Godhead. When He ascended back to heaven he took with him what he did not have in the pre-incarnate state: sinless human nature as an added dimension. Some of the theological discussions in seminary classrooms dealt with the Kenosis, the self-emptying of Christ when he came to earth as a baby human. These discussions also seemed to be disconnected from an historical event in real human lives.

Mom died in 1964. Years before, I had the privilege of leading her in a salvation prayer. It was in the few years remaining in her life that she began to grasp the reality of what the Christmas story meant, and she loved for me to read about it from the Bible when I came home for visits. I began to travel to Israel in 1969, and eventually preached in the Christmas Lutheran Church in Bethlehem, the Nazareth Baptist Church and the Jerusalem Baptist Church as well. I led groups out into the Shepherd's field just east of the town of Bethlehem. There in front of a limestone cave where shepherds have kept their flocks on winter nights for centuries, I have read this Christmas story on numerous occasions. We have prayed many times in the manger cave. We have stood by the site of the Annunciation by Gabriel to Mary in Nazareth. What was the most common response of pilgrims who traveled with me? "This is all real – isn't it!" Of course it is! But how can we get this generation to realize that? How I would have loved to take my mom on one of those pilgrimages. How I would love to take some of those theologians!

You and I must fight a great battle just to keep the reality of Christmas. We are being brainwashed to call it "Season's Greetings" or "Happy Holidays" or just plain "Xmas." It has become a merchant's dream and a poor family's nightmare. In the US, a determined effort by the American Civil Liberties Union in underway to eliminate all mention of Christ and Christmas in any public celebration of this season. (The ACLU was recently incensed when the governor of California renamed the "Holiday Tree" in his mansion. What was the new name that started the firestorm in the media? He intentionally called it the "Christmas Tree!") Public officials are still glad to get their "Christmas" leave, and employees still eagerly look forward to their "Christmas" bonuses. Some retail merchants look to the "Christmas" season for half their annual income. How long will these "perks" continue when our society has erased the memory of the very story that gave rise to the holiday? In today's climate, how can we get people to know the true story?

We must exhibit and teach the heart of the message brought by the angels on that first Christmas. It is wrapped up in one word: *eirene* – the Greek equivalent of the Old Testament word *shalom*. Both mean wholeness, completeness, and wellness. And that is what Christmas brought. The little Jesus grew up to be a big Jesus. He died on the cross so that we could each be reconciled to God. And through him we can have what the angels announced in the first Christmas carol, the very first Christmas greeting: a permanent, personal capsule of peace. That peace will insulate you against the loss of loved ones, against financial disaster, against physical pain and suffering. Because inside that capsule is the grace of God. You must have it before you can communicate it. And when you have it, tell it. Tell it to your children. But then you need to tell children what the little Jesus did for them when he grew up. Then you can say, like Paul Harvey, "And now you know the rest of the story!"

WHAT'S IN THE WELL COMES UP IN THE BUCKET

"Either make the tree good, and his fruit good; or else make the tree corrupt, and his fruit corrupt: for the tree is known by his fruit. O generation of vipers, how can ye, being evil, speak good things? For out of the abundance of the heart the mouth speaketh. A good man out of the good treasure of the heart bringeth forth good things: and an evil man out of the evil treasure bringeth forth evil things." Matthew 12:34-35

"Your speech is a sample of your thoughts. If it's on your mind, it's likely to come up in your conversation. Of course if you never think it, you will never say it."

My boyhood home did not have the luxuries of electricity or running water. We had what we now call "run-and-get-it water." Our sole source of water was a 40-feet-deep dug well in the back yard. As a child one of my chores was to keep the kitchen supplied with fresh buckets of well water. We had a slender tube attached to a rope pulley. Pulling up five buckets for watering the mule, or 20 buckets for filling wash tubs could be hard work. We had a good well – better than some others on neighboring farms. The water was usually clean and cold. On a hot day, nothing tasted better than a drink of cold well water. But there were times it tasted different. Then we would work for an hour or so, attempting to draw all the water out. We would eventually find the source of the new taste: a drowned frog. This was so common in our community that it gave rise to an expression, "What's down in the well comes up in the bucket." The saying meant that if you have something in your heart it will come up in your speech.

That's what Jesus is saying here in verse 34. Out of the abundance of the heart the mouth speaketh. Our words give us away. They reflect a heart condition. That's why we will be held accountable for every word. People may mind their manners when trying to make good impressions, but when they let their guard down, the telltale thoughts come out. "What's down in the well comes up in the bucket." Bitterness, selfishness, worldliness, lewdness, prejudice ... if it's in the heart, it will come out in the speech.

When my daughter began dating, I gave her some advice. I told her to always notice how the young man talked and acted when he was under stress – like having to change a flat tire in the rain. That was a good time to see what he had in his heart. A man nailing shingles on a roof can sometimes shock those around him when he bangs a thumb instead of a nail! Pastoring small churches, I observed that at times of working together, such as during a church property clean-up day on Saturday, some wonderful Sunday Christians say spiteful and hurtful things about others in the church. In an unguarded moment, their speech reveals what is in their hearts.

One of the big problems in today's church fellowship is that it can be so completely superficial. It's all about image and appearance – not about character. People get by in that kind of a relationship because nobody is around them long enough to hear their unguarded thoughts. But spiritual growth is cultivated in an environment of intense interaction between mature and immature believers. Let's remember that who we are in private is who we really are. The persona you project with spiritual jargon is not the real you. Haven't we all heard people whose way of speaking changed immediately when they walked into a church doorway – and nowhere else. "Praise the Lord! God bless you. Glory to God! Hallelujah!" They never talk that way any other place. Have you been guilty of "putting on" at church? But Jesus sees your heart. He knows your thoughts. How humble we all should be before such a holy Person. How much we need to let the Word of God and the presence of Jesus cleanse our hearts! What's down in the well comes up in the bucket! Let's pray today for pure wells.

FRIEND, LET ME TAKE THAT LOAD OFF YOUR SHOULDERS

"Come unto me, all ye that labour and are heavy laden, and I will give you rest." Matthew 11:28

"At almost anytime you are carrying too much on your shoulders. Stop that! It insults the Lord Jesus."

If you've ever had the back pain associated with ruptured discs in your spine, you'll identify with this story. When my son Douglas was a teen, we went on occasional trips to the North Georgia mountains to do some backpacking along whitewater streams. Once I was there with him and a friend, deep in the wilderness, when bad weather struck. Everything was stuffed in our backpacks hurriedly and we began the miles long trek back through rain to where we had parked the car. We didn't have time to evenly distribute the loads and I would up with about 50 pounds – about 15 pounds more than I normally carried. I had my own gear plus a 2-man tent, plus all the food supplies. In my hurry for us to break camp and get on the trail I insisted on tying everything onto my pack. But I wound up with too big a load.

We came to a place where we had to leap down to lower rocks in the trail. The added load and the pull of gravity when I landed on the lower rocks crushed some discs in my back. It hurt some then, but by the time I got home I had to be bedridden. The damage was done and there was no cure. From then on my back bothered me when I did any kind of bending or lifting activity. About five years later, the three discs were permanently fused as the bones grew together and I wound up over an inch shorter in height. I was paying the consequence of carrying too heavy a load.

God has taught me some things about carrying loads that are too heavy. Our bodies were designed with load limits. So were our psyches. There are types of emotional and spiritual loads that are too heavy for you. They weigh you down so that you cannot travel well. They will damage your health. Jesus insists that you let him take the load off your shoulders. He will let you carry another burden instead – one that is easy and light. You probably are so accustomed to carrying all that you do, and think it's all right. But what if you have to jump like I did? Then something in you is going to break. You should let Jesus take your load before that happens.

On one occasion after foot surgery, I traveled on crutches to the mission field. Knowing how awkward it would be to try to handle check-on luggage, I just strapped two carry-on bags around my neck, one over each shoulder. By the time I had shuffled my way down the longest concourse at the Atlanta Airport with those bags swinging on either side and with those straps cutting into my neck, I thought it was the hardest thing I had ever attempted. On arrival at the Cancun airport, I found myself having to negotiate down the steps of the plane, across a hot tarmac, and up more steps to enter the terminal. Then down a long concourse, and more stairs. Then through passport control and customs, all on crutches with those bags around my shoulders. Outside, in the heat, I looked for Alfredo, my Maya friend who was to meet me. He had not arrived. I could not sit down, for then I would not have the strength to get back up. I leaned against a column and waited. And waited! About and hour later, Alfredo arrived. He had been delayed by a flat tire. When he saw me standing there, about to faint, he ran to me.

"Friend, let me take that load off your shoulders," he said. Nothing could have been more welcome. I was so glad to get some help. I did not even think to say as I might have at another time, "No, thank you. I'm fine. It's not heavy. I can handle it." I gladly let him slide those accursed straps off my neck. And then, although I still felt weak and faint, I felt so wonderfully light! It was so great to let go of that load! That's the way you will feel when you truly let Jesus have the load.

It may come as a shock, but the invitation to come to Jesus and let him lighten your load is more than just an invitation. It is a command! And you insult the Lordship of Jesus with your disobedience if you do not do as he says! Imagine telling him, "No, thank you. I'm just fine. I can handle it!" You know you are not just fine. You are at the breaking point. You have to have some relief, just as I did with those bags. This is the time to come to Jesus and let him have your burdens.

YOU'RE NOT HOME YET

"By faith Abraham, when he was called to go out into a place which he should after receive for an inheritance, obeyed; and he went out, not knowing whither he went. By faith he sojourned in the land of promise, as in a strange country, dwelling in tabernacles with Isaac and Jacob, the heirs with him of the same promise: For he looked for a city which hath foundations, whose builder and maker is God." "These all died in faith, not having received the promises, but having seen them afar off, and were persuaded of them, and embraced them, and confessed that they were strangers and pilgrims on the earth. For they that say such things declare plainly that they seek a country. And truly, if they had been mindful of that country from whence they came out, they might have had opportunity to have returned. But now they desire a better country, that is, an heavenly: wherefore God is not ashamed to be called their God: for he hath prepared for them a city." Hebrews 11: 8-10, 13-16

"This world is no longer your home. A Christian ought to feel like an alien in this culture. But we must never forget that we do have a place to call home."

I have learned to live lightly and not to be bound to any earthly territory. I sometimes introduce myself as a pilgrim – "just passing through on my way to heaven." That's the way it was with Abraham. He was rich enough to own a whole city. But he lived in a tent. He remained a pilgrim, knowing he had a home in the city built by God in Heaven. He had the promise of something far better than this world could ever offer him. We need to learn the lesson of living lightly.

On many of my missions overseas I travel alone. No one sees me off at the airport, and no one welcomes me at International Arrivals when I come home. It has become a matter of routine to just leave my vehicle at a park-and-ride place, take the shuttle to the airport, and go to the departure gate alone. Overseas, I am warmly welcomed by cheering church leaders and sometimes even the press. Sometimes they are holding a large welcome banner. I remember on one occasion in Fortaleza, Brazil we were greeted at the airport by about 70 folk, all with identical T-shirts advertising our seminar. They held a large welcome banner. Children dressed in regional costumes presented us flowers. Also, when the missions end, groups of grateful Christians see me off at the airports. But when I come home, there is no such fanfare. On one trip, as I returned through the Atlanta airport, a fellow passenger was greeted by rousing cheers from a large group. Momentarily, I thought, "Why don't people welcome missionaries home like that?" But immediately in my spirit I heard the Lord say, "Son, you're not home yet." That's it exactly: we are not home yet! When we get home to heaven, then we will see the greatest celebration and have the warmest welcome we have ever had!

All of us need occasional reminders that this world is not our home. One of the first times that I can remember that God did this for me was shortly after the death of my mother. I was a young preacher in another state when my mom died from complications of Lupus. Her death hit me particularly hard. I felt so helpless at the graveside as they lowered her casket into the ground. That night I went to bed in the family home there on the farm where I grew up. A flood of memories came over me as I lay there. I thought of the many times I had driven home from Mississippi on visits. I remembered that each time I left, she would come with me to the front gate, and say the same thing every time. She always said, "Hurry home, son!" Then I had a vision of a beautiful arched window – a window in Heaven. Through that window I saw light and heard happy voices. I heard my mother laughing – a rare thing in the last years of her life as she suffered so much pain. And I heard her say, "Hurry home, son." I think God let me have that vision and hear her say that from Heaven, so that I would remember that Heaven was my home. Where I grew up was no longer my home. My real home was there in Heaven.

You and I must learn to live as pilgrims. We are "just passing through on our way to Heaven" as I sometimes remind students on campus. We are on a journey. The journey only ends when we get home to Heaven. Until then, learn to "make do" in a world that is increasingly inhospitable to us. We are not home yet, and our eyes have not yet seen the treasures and pleasures that await us when we get home. Then it will be worth it all. Just remember, you're not home yet!

GETTING READY FOR A STORM

"And said unto them, Sirs, I perceive that this voyage will be with hurt and much damage, not only of the lading and ship, but also of our lives." Acts 27:10; John 16:33

"You will face storms in your life. It is not a matter of if, but when."

In the words of the apostle Paul, your journey will be with much hurt and much damage. Our Lord Jesus has promised us that in the world we will have trouble. But he has also assured us that he has overcome the world. That means everything in it, including all that you will endure. But what can you do to help you survive with less damage?

One afternoon in the Yucatan jungle, I was resting in a hammock inside the grass-thatched hut of a Maya friend. I awakened from my nap to observe my host and some of the men from his village outside talking seriously and pointing at the sky. The sky was clear and the sun was bright, but they were troubled about a change in the weather. They had noticed an unusual southeast wind that was stirring the trees. In a moment they quickly dispersed. Then all of them began to throw ropes over the thatched roofs of their huts and tie them down securely.

Before long, clouds rolled overhead and the wind blew more strongly. Then a hard, driving rain set in. I watched from my hammock as the storm began to blow things away from the clearing. The trees were bent over and their leaves were being stripped from them by the wind. Yet the thatched roof over my dirt floor hut did not move. It was well made to begin with, and now it was tied down with rope. The storm passed over us. I learned later when I returned to town that this was Hurricane Dianne. A class three hurricane, yet all the huts survived with roofs intact. The men had made the right preparations. They did not avoid the storm – they just tied some things down and let it blow. There's a real lesson here. We need to tie some things down in our lives.

Some of you are going on to Seminary. You will encounter some liberal theology. Or, you may attend a church where the pastor does not believe the Bible is complete inspired of God. And you will face a storm of doubt that will challenge your faith. If you are not sure there is a personal God, you need to tie that down. If you are not sure that God really created the universe, you need to tie that down. If you are not sure about the virgin birth and therefore the deity of Jesus, you had better tie that down. If you are not fully convinced that there will be a literal resurrection of your dead body, you had better tie that down.

Study the Word here, not just to gain knowledge, but to settle any possible doubt. Because what is not tied down will surely be blown away. And if you who are ministers have issues of personal doubts, how much more do the people you work with. You must settle all your own doubts so that you can help them settle theirs. Because more than anything else, ministers must teach their people how to weather storms. Let's pray for the Holy Spirit to search our hearts and show us what needs to be tied down.

NECESSITY IS THE MOTHER OF INVENTION AND LEARNING

"And, behold, men brought in a bed a man which was taken with a palsy: and they sought means to bring him in, and to lay him before him. And when they could not find by what way they might bring him in because of the multitude, they went upon the housetop, and let him down through the tiling with his couch into the midst before Jesus." Luke 5: 18-19

"Desperation brings motivation; motivation brings creativity; creativity brings solutions."

You have to admire these four men who brought a sick friend to Jesus in Capernaum. The crowd was so huge; they could not get to Jesus by ordinary means. But the Scripture says, "They sought means to bring him in..." That must mean that they tried other ideas. Nothing worked. But finally they came up with the plan that did work. Had they been less determined, they would have given up in failure. *Necessity is the mother of invention.* I remember several times of desperate necessity in my life. Those were the moments of breakthrough for me. I would pray and try to think "outside the box," and God would show me a way out of my difficulty. In those times, God shaped me for becoming the visionary He would later require me to be. The lessons were small at first. For instance, when I was on my first archeological dig in Israel we were working in a hot, dry desert. I was surrounded by Hebrew-speaking Israelis who did not understand English. I had not yet learned to speak a single sentence in Hebrew. There I was, working the first day in the desert sun, dehydrating and not knowing even how to ask for a drink of water.

But I listened and heard someone else say the word "mayam" in connection with a clay water pipe we had unearthed. I also heard dig supervisors asking for tools in Hebrew, prefacing their request with the phrase "ten lee." I understood it to mean "give me." Another word I heard on several occasions was "b'vahkeshah." I made that out to be "please." From those fragments, I constructed my first Hebrew sentence. I climbed down the mound and went to the mess tent. I entered and said, "Ten lee mayam, b'vahkeshah." (Give me water, please.) It worked and I not only got my water, but I began to learn a language.

If we can do such things in the natural, how much more can we accomplish with prayer and the wisdom of God's Holy Spirit? The Lord always has a solution. And He tells us, "You have not because you ask not." Usually, lack of sufficient desperation is the reason we don't ask. If you are truly desperate, you will pray. And when you pray, God turns the little idea "light bulb" on inside your head. How many times have you been working on a stubborn car, tractor, or lawn mower that wouldn't start and reached that desperation point? And when you did, you prayed for God to show you how to fix it. And when He did, did you learn anything? I have learned over the years that God knows all about mechanical problems! And He has taught me so much that sometimes I diagnose a problem in a car before a professional mechanic does.

The point is this: you will never know much more than you know now if you do not get sufficiently motivated by some kind of desperation. Was your decision to come to Bible college mostly just a whim, or was it born out of necessity? Do you hunger and thirst for knowledge of the Word of God like you would for food and water? If not, the first few difficulties you face here might be enough to convince you to give up. But if as Paul says in I Corinthians 9:16, a necessity has been laid upon you, then you cannot stop until you have the proper training to preach. A story is told that a student once approached Socrates and asked, "What is the secret to becoming a good learner?" Whereupon, Socrates grabbed the student and forced his face into the water of a nearby fountain. He held him there until he almost drowned; then released him. Gasping for air, the student protested. Socrates then calmly said, "When you desire knowledge as greatly as you desired air just then, you will be a good learner."

The four friends of the paralytic sought for means, and they found means by which to bring their friend to Jesus. If you pray and search hard enough, you will find means to meet the financial requirements. You will find means to deal with all the other challenges such as, daycare for children, time in your schedule for the classes you need, tutoring in typing skills, and even the necessary transportation. Seek seriously for means, and you will find a way. If you don't understand an assignment, and you desperately want to do well in this school, you will seek for means to get the help you need. Necessity is a good teacher. It teaches you to pray. It teaches you to look at all your options. It teaches you to be creative. It teaches you to succeed.

MAY I HELP YOU, PLEASE?

"Bear ye one another's burdens, and so fulfil the law of Christ." "A new commandment I give unto you, That ye love one another; as I have loved you, that ye also love one another." "And this is the confidence that we have in him, that, if we ask any thing according to his will, he heareth us: And if we know that he hear us, whatsoever we ask, we know that we have the petitions that we desired of him." Galatians 6:2; John 13:34; I John 5:14,15

"Everyone needs miracles. In an atmosphere of faith, miracles can happen routinely. Therefore, everyone should seriously seek an atmosphere of faith in God."

The Word here in Galatians says that we should bear other people's burdens. It says we fulfill the law of Christ when we do that! The law of Christ is that we should love one another. That's explicitly said by our Lord in John 13. But love must be expressed in action or it is not love – only a sentiment. When Christians truly love one another with the love of Christ, they pray for one another. If they love a person, they are sensitive to the burdens of heart and mind that the other person may be carrying, and they help lift those burdens through prayer. We are told here in I John 5 that prayers which are prayed with confidence bring answers. Prayers are more effective when several or many believers all believe the same thing. That's what we call an atmosphere of faith!

In the mid-seventies, while I served as pastor of Our Shepherd's Church, we sought to extend this burden-bearing concept to the body of Christ at large through a radio broadcast. It was a call-in program, so that the audience could hear live calls from Christians making prayer requests, and then hear us pray with them over the phone. We created an atmosphere of faith for the listener in three ways. First, we read over the air a faith-building scripture passage as we began each broadcast. Secondly, we received live call-in reports from people with whom we had previously prayed. Those were often electrifying! Thirdly, we asked all listening Christians to concentrate their prayers with us as we prayed for each caller.

The name of our program was "May I Help You, Please?" Those were the first words we said to each caller. Countless miracles resulted from the broadcast. We often had several calls at the beginning of the program from people who testified about miracles God had done for them after they called us and received prayer the previous week. Word spread quickly, and our audience grew. The broadcast was done by a remote loop from our church office to the radio station. Our phone system could only handle six lines at a time, and we had three or four volunteers fully occupied taking calls throughout the 30-minute broadcast. When, for instance, someone who had been blind began to see, the phones jammed for the rest of the day – long after we were off the air.

In this tremendous atmosphere of faith, I sometimes found myself being strangely moved by the Holy Spirit to say things I would not normally say over the radio. In one broadcast, I began by reading the scripture and inviting people to call in who wanted to report results from previous broadcasts. Then, as we were taking those calls, I stopped in the middle of a conversation over the air and said, "I believe I have a word of knowledge that is a message to someone who has to hear it right now." I went on to say that in my mind I had a picture of a man driving a green pickup, going north on a highway, listening to the broadcast at that moment. I said I felt he had just had a bad argument with his wife, and he felt like his marriage was over. I went on to say that he was approaching a bridge, and across the bridge was a phone booth. I said that he had a quarter in his pocket, and that God wanted him to stop and make a phone call to us. I gave him the number and told him that God was going to put his life back together. In a moment, one of the workers came over from the phones and whispered, wide-eyed, "It's the man in the pickup!"

I knew something awesome in the spiritual realm was taking place. I took the call and the audience heard a man on the other end of the phone line say shakily, "It's me! It's me!" He had just had an argument with his wife; he was traveling north in a green pickup; as he heard me speak there was a phone booth just over a bridge, and he had only a quarter in his pocket! I was amazed, and he was hardly able to speak. He wanted to surrender his heart to Christ and be saved, so I led him in a brief prayer to receive Christ's forgiveness and lordship. I then told him to go find someone who would listen and immediately confess that he had surrendered to Christ. I also instructed him to seek out a pastor of a church near his home and also confess to him. I shared that he would need to be baptized as soon as possible, and that he should trust God to heal his marriage. He thanked me and the call ended.

One week later, during a Wednesday night service in our church, a group of young adult visitors came in. As they were being seated, one of them identified himself as Billy Pope, the man in the green pickup who had called in the week before. He told me he was from Locust Grove, and that he had sought out a local pastor who happened to be an acquaintance of mine, Don Pye. After hearing his testimony, Don had baptized him just three days ago. Billy then introduced me to his wife. She had gotten saved when she heard Billy's story, and Don had baptized them together! Then Billy introduced me to another couple. In the weeks before Billy and his wife got saved, they had fallen out with the other couple. The argument had reached the point that they made death threats against one another. But when the second couple heard about what God had done for Billy, they received Christ too, and here they were, sitting in our church. But there were two more people with Billy that night. Billy went on to say that they also had gotten saved on the weekend after they heard Billy's testimony. So, there they were: six newly saved souls who had come to bear testimony to the power of God.

The atmosphere of faith created by the large broadcast audience was birthed out of our ministry team. But that effect in turn increased interest in our church services and built attendance. The wonderful thing about the new members who resulted from the radio broadcast was that they came with faith, expecting to see similar works of God in our church services. And because they came with such expectations, they helped strength even more the atmosphere of faith in our church. During the middle seventies, that church experienced a lengthy season of weekly and sometimes daily miracles. Healing miracles were common. We saw transvestites, alcoholics and drug addicts completely delivered. Financial miracles came to many families. People were saved and filled with the Holy Spirit in every service.

I challenge you, dear reader, to start today building an atmosphere of faith in your own ministry. If you are not a ministry leader at present, I urge you to seek out a ministry that has an atmosphere of faith, and join it. God is looking for believers who have confidence in His Word, and who will pray accordingly. You need miracles, but you will receive them most often when you are bearing someone else's burden. Hook up with others who are unselfish and just love people enough to pray for them. That's the kind of people who often say, "May I help you, please?"!

SHOULD YOU EVEN WANT TO BE HAPPY?

"Blessed are the poor in spirit: for theirs is the kingdom of heaven. Blessed are they that mourn: for they shall be comforted. Blessed are the meek: for they shall inherit the earth. Blessed are they which do hunger and thirst after righteousness: for they shall be filled. Blessed are the merciful: for they shall obtain mercy. Blessed are the pure in heart: for they shall see God. Blessed are the peacemakers: for they shall be called the children of God. Blessed are they which are persecuted for righteousness' sake: for theirs is the kingdom of heaven. Blessed are ye, when men shall revile you, and persecute you, and shall say all manner of evil against you falsely, for my sake." Matthew 5:3-11

"You can be happy without being blessed. But why would you want to? Only in blessedness is contentment, peace, fulfillment and joy. "

Happiness and blessedness are often taken to be the same. They are not. The Greek word for happiness, *eudaimon*, does not appear in the Bible; nor does the word for its equivalent *eutuches* (good luck). Happiness depends on happenstance, or luck. Blessedness, praise God, does not! The word for blessed appears many times in the Bible: first as *esher* in the Hebrew and then as *makarioi* in the Greek. It describes a joyful mental state of contentment arising from true comfort and security. My son Douglas as a teenager had a classmate who was the son of a millionaire. He spent a weekend in as a guest in the millionaire's home. Afterward he said to me with wisdom beyond his years, "Dad, there's just no correlation between having money and being happy." And he was right. But the problem is that people grow up in our society conditioned to think that wealth brings happiness. And that expectation guarantees failure, disappointment, and depression.

In this passage Jesus is giving the inaugural address of his earthly ministry, laying down the laws of his kingdom. Beginning with verse 3, he describes blessedness (Gr. *makariotes*). The key is the phrase in verse 11, "...for my sake." We can only be blessed when we are indwelt by the Spirit of Christ, and experience God's nature in us. That is how we can have the kingdom of God within us. From verse 3 through verse 11 he is giving us the steps by which we arrive at true blessedness. Our blessedness depends upon the fulfillment of the conditions that Jesus sets forth here in the Beattitudes. The first step to blessedness is to become poor in spirit – meaning that we realize our spiritual helplessness. The second step is to mourn, that is, to have sorrow for one's sins. That is a passive attitude. The third step changes the attitude to active: we must exhibit "meekness" which is from the Greek word *prautes*. In the context it means to become angry at sin.

The fourth step is to hunger for God's righteousness

(*dikaiosune*) which is what God expects us to do. The present tense participle here allows the sense of "hungering ones" – meaning that we are constantly hungry for more, even though constantly satisfied with the realization of God's righteousness in our lives. The fifth step is an outward demonstration of the Christlike characteristic, mercifulness. This is from the Greek *eleos*. This is the godly character trait of empathy with the unbeliever and suffering with him the consequences of his sin and doing whatever we can to relieve him from sin's tragic results.

Mercy is wonderful but it is no substitute for grace. Grace comes only from God and can affect character and change it. Mercy cannot change character but focuses only on allievia-tion of the consequences of sinful character. Step six is purity of heart. This comes as a continuous cleansing. God's grace working on your character from his presence within produces at first a sense of spiritual helplessness (poor in spirit); then second, a mourning over your sinfulness; then third, an anger at sin; then fourth, hungriness for righteousness; then fifth, mercifulness; then eighth, purity. The more pure a person becomes, the clearer will be his sight of God.

The seventh step is peacemaking: not simply trying to patch up relationships, but bringing the peace of God that you have experienced into the lives of others. The eighth step is persecution for righteousness which causes you to reach the very highest rung of the ladder of satisfaction – because it brings you into the most perfect conformity with the Lord who suffered for you. So it may be that you have been looking for something called happiness and you never will find it. You should be looking for blessedness, and you have already started enjoying it. From here on, it will only increase. Once the fire is kindled on the hearth, you no longer search for a match. When you are joyful you no longer need to be happy.

THIS IS A TIME
TO TRIM LAMPS

"And at midnight there was a cry made, Behold, the bridegroom cometh; go ye out to meet him. Then all those virgins arose, and trimmed their lamps." Matthew 25:6-7

"An untrimmed lamp is a sorry thing to see with. You stumble a lot with an untrimmed lamp."

Jesus was giving a parable about preparation for the Second Coming. Parables rely upon vivid word pictures to convey key ideas. This parable is the one we call the Parable of the Ten Virgins. The Bridegroom came at a dark time. Lamps were needed. Not just any lamps, but bright lamps. Because the Bridegroom was long in coming, the oil in the lamps was used up, and the wicks were crusted with soot. The flame, if any, was now quite dim. But when the announcement came at midnight, all the virgins got up and trimmed their lamps. How did they do that? What did that involve?

Let me take you back to a time in my youth when the lights

in my farm home were oil lamps. These were kerosene lamps with glass globes – a better light than the oil lamps made of clay in the parable. But they used the same principle: a burning wick soaked in oil from the reservoir. As our lamps burned every night, the globes gradually blackened with soot from the smoking flame. The wicks slowly crusted with carbon. As the oldest son, I had outside chores and inside chores each evening. My inside chores included drawing water from the well, gathering firewood, and trimming the lamps. I hated trimming the lamps.

Each evening I took the same three lamps out to the front steps where I could see best in the gathering twilight. There I would take an old rag and wipe the inside of each glass globe until it was clean again. It was a dirty job. I would refill each lamp with oil. Then I would take scissors and carefully cut away the carbonized tip of each wick. Then one by one, I would strike a match and re-light each wick and replace each globe, and adjust the flame. Then I would carry the brightly shining lamps back into the darkening house.

The chore that the virgins had to perform for their lamps was only slightly simpler than was mine as a boy. They did not have to bother with globes. But three things were necessary: oil, wick and flame. They had to have enough oil. The wick in the lamp was a picture of our life: we cannot produce the flame of witness unless we draw upon the oil of the Holy Spirit. When the night is the darkest, we need the brightest light. That is why we must trim the wick – cut away the deposits of sin and worldliness.

While you are in training here, it is time to trim lamps. Some stuff will have to be cut away so that your light will be brighter. And you will need a fresh supply of oil. And you will need some inspiration to ignite a new flame. Each of these involves a determined commitment on your part. It's painful to cut away part of your life. You will be tempted not to. It's hard to admit that you're low on oil. You will be tempted to pretend you're okay. And it may take someone else's help to relight your flame. But your lamp of witness must stay bright. Trim it and keep on trimming it. You dare not let it go out. Jesus is coming!

BUILDING ABOVE THE STARS

"Lay not up for yourselves treasures upon earth, where moth and rust doth corrupt, and where thieves break through and steal: But lay up for yourselves treasure in heaven, where neither moth nor rust doth corrupt, and where thieves do not break through nor steal." Matthew 6:19-20

"If what you have built for yourself can be taken away from you, then you have been building too low."

I was still a young man, just getting started in the ministry when God spoke to me in a most unusual place. I was speaking at a Gideon convention in Detroit. While there, I thought it would be interesting to take a bus ride through the tunnel under the river and go over to the Canadian side. As I rode along in the tunnel, for some reason I found myself thinking about my future. I wanted to make sure that I was in the right calling. At that moment I looked up in the ceiling of the bus and saw a placard which said, "They build too low who build beneath the stars." It jolted my senses to read such a message precisely at the time I was thinking those thoughts! It could not have been mere coincidence that I would see that statement at precisely that moment. That placard was unlike the dozen or so others of the same size posted inside the bus. They all advertised some product or service. But this sign only said, "They build too low who build beneath the stars." Here I was, deep in a tunnel under a river; yet I knew I was seeing a message from God. I have never forgotten it.

Looking back across nearly fifty years of ministry, I'm very glad that years ago I chose to follow Christ; preferring spiritual riches over worldly wealth. Since that time I have seen many "successful" careers end in disaster. I have seen men build their entire life upon attaining material prestige and comfort. And I have seen their entire worlds crash with the loss of their job or company. They were building too low. Jesus taught that we are to lay up treasure where we can never lose it: in heaven. If all that we possess is on earth, then moth and rust will corrupt it, or thieves will steal it. Over the years I have invested in imperishable things like the souls of men, the knowledge of God's Word, joy in the presence of the Savior and the glory of the Kingdom of God. No thief can ever steal that.

When my family lived on Lee Street in Decatur, we had a

row of hedge that ran the length of the front of our home. One spring day I noted a sparrow building her nest in the hedge. I thought, "She's building too low." Sure enough, a few weeks later, I heard her distraught calls and looked out my bedroom window. There was a snake in the bush, devouring the eggs in the sparrow's nest. She had built too low. We must guard against settling for the comforts of this life. We must build for a future beyond the stars. As the chorus goes, "The world behind me, the cross before me. No turning back, no turning back." Too many ministers answer the call and then turn back; becoming interested in such things as their "package" and salary more than the things of God. Jesus warned, "Remember Lot's wife." She looked back and could never go forward again.

Have you made up your mind to sacrifice everything if that is what it costs to follow Jesus? Do you really believe His promise that if you do, you will have treasure in Heaven? What does the concept of Heaven mean to you? Is it so real to you that nothing else matters? Take a mental survey of your life. Where does your best energy and most of your time go? I trust it is focused on things that will last forever. May God give you the grace and faith to know that your destiny is beyond the stars, and the wisdom to live accordingly.

BEING ALL YOU CAN BE

"And to know the love of Christ, which passeth knowledge, that ye might be filled with all the fullness of God. Now unto him that is able to do exceeding abundantly above all that we ask or think, according to the power that worketh in us," Ephesians 3:19-20

"We can never fulfill some of our childhood dreams. But there are some God-given potentials that we can fulfill. That's the real world for me now."

This text in verse 19 says "...that ye might be filled with all the fullness of God." The phrase, "filled with all the fullness" is a translation of one Greek word: *pleroma*. It means that an entire capacity is completely filled. That's reaching your potential! In verse 20 we see that God is "...able to do exceeding abundantly above all that we ask or think ..." The Greek term for exceeding abundantly is *huperekperissou*. The prefix *huper* makes it very emphatic: God is able to do far more with us that we can possibly imagine!

When I was a child I wanted to be all sorts of things for which I would never have the ability or the opportunity. When adults heard me speak of these things some of them just smiled. Others chuckled over my great ambitions. They knew I could never do those things. But since I have met Christ, I have discovered that God can do some amazing things with me – and I get the impression that he wants to do more. The new creation that I have become has potentialities through Christ that I never thought of as a child; potentialities that I do not yet fully understand.

We all admire those who stretch their limits, develop their

potentials and achieve greatness. But each of us have potentials for different destinies. I can never do with a baseball bat what Hank Aaron could do. I can never do with a golf club what Tiger Woods can do. I can never do what Michaelangelo did with a paintbrush. I can never do what Albert Einstein did in physics. But I can do things they cannot. My potential lies in a different area. But we all have one thing in common. We have to work hard to develop our potential – to become all we can be!

Whatever it is that God has planned for you to become, will you let God fulfill that in you? Ephesians 2:10 says, "For we are his workmanship, created in Christ Jesus unto good works, which God hath before ordained that we should walk in them." God has a special plan for your life. You need to forget childish dreams and forget worldly ambitions. If you have just answered God's call, you also need to forget what you think you are already equipped for. Let God show you how he likes to use you. Let him show you the new direction. Then focus on it and work on it.

Dream about it. Think about it. Talk about it. And stay at it. Day after day, discipline yourself so that you can be all that you can be. If God has called you to preach, don't go at it half-heartedly. Study. Put time in your preparation. Polish your delivery. Hide God's messages in your heart and be prepared! If God has called you to teach, train and train some more, to be the best teacher you can be. If God has called you to write, work at it. If God has called you into a service ministry, work hard and make that ministry the greatest one you have ever seen.

Most of you here have been sent here by God, and you have been destined for greatness. But whether you will be all that you can be is up to you alone. Can you set aside other pursuits? Can you focus? Can you dream of greater potential? Can you put in the required work to be all that you can be?

WHEN YOUR FLIGHT PLANS ARE INTERRUPTED

"And when it was day, they knew not the land: but they discovered a certain creek with a shore, into the which they were minded, if it were possible, to thrust in the ship. And when they had taken up the anchors, they committed themselves unto the sea, and loosed the rudder bands, and hoisted up the mainsail to the wind, and made toward shore." Acts 27:39-40

"There are times when your flight plan is interrupted and all you can think about is a safe place to land. Even then God is in charge."

The captain of Paul's ship had a plan for the voyage, but a storm changed his plan. At first they had no hope of surviving. Then they found land. They didn't even know where they were, but any land would do. They found a small shore and made toward it. On the island, God performed miracles through Paul. It was obvious God was in charge all along.

In the mid-70's I traveled to some speaking engagements in

a private single-engine plane, flown by a church member who was a good pilot. This pilot friend was a careful man and always filed our flight plans. One day we were on our way from Atlanta to Monroe, Louisiana. We ran into a strong headwind around Jackson, Mississippi and by the time we reached the Mississippi River the engine was struggling so hard to keep airspeed against that headwind that our fuel reserve began to quickly drop. In fact, it looked for a long while like we were poised in the air over the river, not making any progress. We got the definite feeling that something sinister in that headwind was trying to destroy us. We began looking for a safe place to land, but there was none. Finally, the fuel ran out.

It is a serious enough problem when you run out of gas in a car on the interstate. But I can tell you that it is far more serious when you run out of gas in the air! To make it more serious, we had crossed the river and were now over a cloud bank. It was raining beneath us. We could not see what type of terrain might be under us. My pilot said, matter-of-factly, "We are going to have to set her down." With the engine sputtering on the last drops of precious fuel, he put the Cessna into a gliding descent.

Then he asked, "You are from this area. What kind of land is down there?" I interrupted my prayers long enough to say, "Either swamps with cypress trees, or cotton fields." "Pray for cotton!" he said as we entered the cloud. I said, "Let's pray for a runway too!" (I didn't like the idea of crash landing even in an open field!) God gave us cotton. As we broke below the cloud at about 100 feet, we could see through the rain that we were skimming just above rows of cotton stalks. That alone was a miracle from God. But wait, God gave us even more! Just in front of us was the end of a crop-duster's runway. We landed and taxied silently to within feet of the hanger shed.

It was in middle of a huge field. On such a rainy day, there would be no one around to help us. However, in the shed there was a parked Ag-Cat crop duster plane. We siphoned about five gallons of fuel, left a note of apology and our home phone numbers – and a couple of twenties on the pilot's seat, and got airborne again. We made it to the Monroe airport where we were taken by car to the revival service. God mightily used us in the meeting. We had planned that trip with meticulous attention to detail. We knew exactly what cities we would fly over, where we would land, how many hours and how much fuel we would use. Our plans got interrupted, but God was in charge.

That was the first time I was in a small plane that ran out of gas. But it was not the last time. On the return flight from that same trip to Monroe, it happened again. Once more, it was not pilot error, but unexpected weather. Again, we filed a flight plan. This time, however, a rotating tropical depression had moved in, and now on the back side of the storm we faced another powerful headwind. Again, I sensed the Devil himself in that storm, trying to kill us. To make matters worse, now it was night. As we began to run low on fuel, we determined not to get caught and have to make another emergency landing.

We got on the radio between Birmingham and Atlanta and

tried to locate a lighted airfield. We were not close enough to the nearest one. There was one on our flight path about half an hour ahead in West Georgia. We would have only enough fuel to get that far. Yet when the fuel needle reached empty, we could not find the lights of the airfield. We prayed earnestly, and finally, as we tilted the nose down to crash land, we saw the lights! My pilot did not think we would reach the runway. He sent out a "Mayday!" on the radio. I prayed. The plane stayed aloft just long enough to touch down safely on the runway. By this time, I was praising the Lord with all my might!

We were behind some hills and could not raise any response on the radio to give the obligatory "All-Clear" on the Mayday. It was about 2 AM and everything at the airport was locked up. No one was around to help us make a phone call. But within minutes a county sheriff's deputy arrived to check on the Mayday call. He was an understanding person who helped us siphon more borrowed gas from a parked plane. We again left a note of thanks and some money. It was 7 AM when I made it safely home again. We had our plans, but those plans had been interrupted twice on the same trip.

Here's a huge life lesson. We have plans, but God has *the* plan. God is in charge of every moment of our lives. Our priorities may change in a moment of crisis. We may have to forget all our previous plans. God never has to make such an adjustment. The sudden turns in our lives are not sudden to God. Keep that in mind during your next crisis and see what God will do.

YOU CAN'T STAY ON AUTOPILOT FOREVER

"Then answered Peter, and said unto Jesus, Lord, it is good for us to be here: If thou wilt, let us make here three tabernacles; one for thee, and one for Moses, and one for Elijah." Matthew 17:4

"There are moments of bliss which you wish could last forever. But soon afterward you must deal with the cold realities of life. We can be so heavenly minded we are of no earthly good to anyone."

There's nothing like the experience of flying low over the Caribbean on a beautiful day. We were returning from Haiti by way of Providentiales Island in the Grand Turks. I had settled into the co-pilot seat of a twin engine Beechcraft. Five Haitians were seated in back. I knew the pilot from previous flights. As we leveled off after takeoff from Cape Haitian, he confided to me that he was bone-weary. He had been flying round the clock for 24 hours, picking up and dropping off new planes for his company.

He was to pick up another new plane on Providentiales, and he had to study the operation manual for that plane during this flight. Since for the next hour and 45 minutes we had a straight flight over open water, he set the plane on autopilot and began to study his notebook. In a few minutes, I saw him nodding. He fell asleep. I did not have a pilot's license, although I had taken some pilot training. I knew the instrument panel fairly well. I saw the plane was flying well on autopilot. I wondered how long he might doze, so I remained quiet.

For over one hour, I watched the skies for other aircraft and monitored the instrument panel. The pilot continued to sleep. That hour was extraordinarily calm and peaceful. The engines droned on steadily. The water beneath us was a transparent turquoise and the sky above was azure blue. God was giving me a special time alone with him. To me it seemed like God was flying the plane. I didn't want that time to end, but I saw on the radar that we were approaching a land mass. The time out was about one hour and 15 minutes. I knew we should get ready to land, so I nudged my sleeping friend.

He awakened with a start, saw the situation and was obviously embarrassed. I reassured him and explained I had been watching while we were autopilot. I had only awakened him because it was time to land. I promised I would keep our little adventure a secret. He immediately busied himself with a dozen tasks that had to be attended to as we prepared to land. The magical moment was over and we were once again dealing with the cold realities of flying.

Your life as a Christian is like that. You can have some wonderful experiences in which you have nothing to do but just go along for the ride. And God just blesses you and blesses you. That's wonderful, isn't it? You wish you could stay in that mode forever. But all too soon you have to deal with life as it really is. You can't stay on autopilot forever.

Peter wanted to stay on the mountain where they had seen

the transfiguration of Jesus, and witnessed the appearance of Moses and Elijah. He wanted to build tabernacles there and just stay. They wouldn't have to do anything. Just watch. This was great! But Jesus had already started down the mountain. At the foot of the mountain was a distraught father whose son was possessed of a demon. He needed help – help Jesus could give only if he left the mountain top.

Here you are at the point of a new challenge in your life. No matter what kind of wonderful experiences you have had where God did it all and you just watched, here you will have to work. You're not on autopilot. College students soon find out that the books won't read themselves. The A's won't automatically appear on your record. God will help you, as Jesus helped the disciples at the foot of the mountain. But you will have to participate in the work. There's a time to sleep and there's a time to just watch God do it all. But then there's a time to wake up and go to work. I think you know what time it is!

DESPERATELY NEEDING LIGHT

"Then fearing lest we should have fallen upon rocks, they cast four anchors out of the stern, and wished for the day." Acts 27:29

"There are times when it's too dark. You wish for light so you can see the dangers around you. Fear starts to rule your life. What do you do?"

Paul was in the dark like all his shipmates. But he didn't have to wish for daylight as desperately as they did. He had received a promise from God that they would all be spared and he believed it. I like to read the promises of God in the Bible. They have helped me face many a dark time. But sometimes a fear strikes us so swiftly we have no time to study any scriptures. I was leading a Holy Land tour and we were visiting the pyramid of Sakkara in Egypt. This is the oldest pyramid and it has a stairway descending about 150 feet down under the center of the pyramid. There are some marvelous old hieroglyphics on the walls of its underground chambers. The steps were steep and we had some seniors, so I had the group wait. I went down first to assess whether they could safely negotiate the stairs and the low headway. The female guide accompanied me with a flashlight.

The stairs were in good condition, and the glyphs on the wall were magnificent – almost 5,000 years old. I sent the guide back for the group. Being out of shape, I didn't want to make an unnecessary trip back up those stairs. Being a gentleman, I let her take the flashlight. I assured her I could just wait there in the dark until she returned. I sat down beside a stone column. When the light disappeared back up the stairway, I found myself encased in a smothering darkness and absolute silence.

Suddenly I heard steps and a rustling sound, just on the other side of the column. I didn't imagine it. Someone was there! I really could have used that flashlight about then. A match flared and then I saw in its light the face of an elderly

Egyptian. Without a word, he lit a lantern and sat down by it. It turned out that he was the caretaker. To conserve his precious kerosene he only burned the lantern when guests were present. I had no idea that there was another human being in that pyramid!

Can you imagine the thoughts that flashed into my mind? When I was a boy, I saw dozens of horror movies about mummies in pyramids! How do you keep from having a heart attack in a moment like that? If you haven't dislodged all those childhood fears by revisiting them with the sound mind of a child of God, you may still have some lurking and waiting for just such a moment. But what about adult fears? Even Christians can lose their peace with God and wind up in a nightmare of fear as they face cancer or heart surgery.

The answer is to intensely internalize not only the Word of God but the presence of God. The earlier you can do this in life, the better. Then as you face the unexpected and the unknown, you will be too close to God to be afraid of anything. Are you facing some fear? We are not children of the night, but of the day. In fact we are the light of the world. As long as God is shining in our hearts, no terror can grip us! While you study for your courses, why not also purpose to maximize your devotional time with God. "Intensely internalize not only the Word of God, but his presence as well."

AS LONG AS GOD SINGS

"And he is before all things, and by him all things consist."

"But the heavens and the earth, which are now, by the same word are kept in store, reserved unto fire against the day of judgment and perdition of ungodly men." "But the day of the Lord will come as a thief in the night; in the which the heavens shall pass away with a great noise, and the elements shall melt with fervent heat, the earth also and the works that are therein shall be burned up." "But none saith, Where is God my maker, who giveth songs in the night;" "When the morning stars sang together, and all the sons of God shouted for joy?" Colossians 1:17; 2 Peter 3:7, 10; Job 35:10; 38:7

I strongly suspect that every thing in our physical world is generated by a song that God began to sing in creation and continues to sing to this day. I wonder what will happen to us when that song stops.

In the old hymn, "This is My Father's World," the first line reflects a profound truth. It says, "This is my father's world, and to my listening ears, all natures sings, and round me rings the music of the spheres." What the song writer Maltbie D. Babcock knew by faith, science is now beginning to describe. A recent program on the public television program Nova discussed something called the "String Theory." It was the obsession Albert Einstein worked on ceaselessly until his death. This particular program caught my attention because I have long believed that every physical thing exists by an ongoing word from the Creator. I think that the material universe is not matter as we know it; but when reduced down to the smallest parts of atoms, everything is really made of tiny bundles of energy created by the voice of God.

I've always been fascinated by the notion taught by science that within the atom, the little electrons and protons that chase each other around in orbits are really negative and positive charges of energy. Where did that energy come from? Every effect must have a cause. Most scientists now agree that the universe itself started out of nothing with a "Big Bang." Of course the explanation of science stops there, since it is difficult to conceive of any cause that could exist outside of time and space. On the Nova program I learned that new discoveries have led to the theory that all things are made of tiny little "strings" of vibrating energy. These energy strings exist at the level of the smallest units within atoms. They also exist in the most powerful forces known to science such as gravity, electromagnetism, and radiation. They are the basic components of material existence!

The new theory seeks to unify all types of energy into one formula statement. Until now, there had not been much thought about the electromagnetic energy outside of atoms being the same energy within the atom that is described by quantum mechanics. In fact, until now, the scientific community has been unable to tie all energy types together. There are many different types of energy known to science: gravity, electromagnetism, sound waves, light waves, radiation, and many more. But these energies have one thing in common: they are all perpetual pulses of vibrating energy! Some unheard sound is causing the energy strings to vibrate. Imagine that! God is singing, and the "music of the spheres" is really the reverberating harmony of trillions of "strings!"

The scriptures we have just read hint at the fact that God sings, and that His songs are related to Creation. As long as God sings, the strings that make up all atoms will continue to give their music and the universe will continue. But when He stops, and those little vibrating strings of heavenly music grow silent, the world as we know it will end. That's how awesome God is. Our worldview, Christian theism, says that God operates from outside of time and space. That's His transcendence! But our worldview also says that God also operates within time and space. That's His immanence!

Think about it! If the voice of God maintains the stars in space and all that you see on earth, how much more does His voice resonate within the body of a believer. The transcendent God comes to us through the new birth and dwells in us in the form of the Holy Spirit. His Spirit creates a harmony in your life. That harmony lessens conflict and increases agreement with the greater chorus of Creation. That's the peace, or shalom of God, that the angels sang about on that first Christmas night! Do you have this harmony in your heart? As long as God sings, you live in the day of opportunity. But when the music stops, it will be the end of the age. Everything that is material will melt away in the fire of judgment. But that which is spiritual will continue. Let's get our minds on the heavenly things which are eternal, and concern ourselves less with the temporary things of this earth. Pray today for the harmony of God in your life.

Part Three

MORE LIFE EXPERIENCES THAT CHANGED ME

WHAT ON EARTH IS
THE DASH FOR?

"So teach us to number our days, that we may apply our hearts unto wisdom." "Then shall the dust return to the earth as it was: and the spirit shall return unto God who gave it." "But God commendeth his love toward us, in that, while we were yet sinners, Christ died for us." "And that he died for all, that they which live should not henceforth live unto themselves, but unto him which died for them, and rose again." "That being justified by his grace, we should be made heirs according to the hope of eternal life." Psalms 90:12; Ecclesiastes 12:7; Romans 5:8; 2 Corinthians 5:15; Titus 3:7

"On my gravesite they will put my date of birth and my date of death. In between there will be a dash. That dash represents my whole life on earth. But what on earth is it for?"

Have you seen any photos lately that show yourself as you were 10 years ago? What's happening to you? It means you are living out your life. The years are passing all too quickly. Are you quite sure you are using your lifetime for the purposes God intended? Recently I went back to my childhood community in Louisiana and spoke at the old Mount Pleasant Church homecoming service. I left that community 48 years earlier, but a flood of memories made it seem like yesterday. Out there in the cemetery were the graves of many of my relatives as well as many neighbors I had known as a boy. A whole community that once was there was now gone from this world. Observing that the inscriptions only showed a dash between the birth and death dates, I spoke on the subject "What On Earth Is The Dash For?"

I am convinced that we are put on earth to find out what we were put on earth for. Then we are to use our window of time on earth to accomplish that. The five verses just read sum up the Bible's explanation of what that little dash between birth and death is for. We must number our days and apply our hearts to wisdom, because soon our spirit will leave and our body will return to dust. God loves us and Christ has died for us so that by His grace we can be forgiven of our ungodliness and live the rest of our lives for Christ. That our universe is not eternal is now an accepted fact, one recognized by the scientific community. The universe had a beginning, and it is now wearing out. Before the beginning of time and space, there was a time when there was no time and no space. That means that the scientific community now agrees that this universe is an effect which had a cause. Several leading scientists such as Carl Sagan, Stephen Hawkins, George Smoot and Fred Hoyle go as far as to refer to intelligent design in the universe. Some even speak of the "anthropic principle," meaning that such factors as the expansion rate, stellar radiation, resonance of the carbon atom, and gravity are all carefully fine-tuned for the existence of man. Only a few will publicly admit that the Cause might be a transcendent God who exists beyond time and space. Their explanation of existence stops short of going back to what caused the Big Bang.

But the Bible, God's self-revelation to us, clearly states in its first line that in the beginning, He created the heavens and the earth. And the first man, Adam, writing in the first book ever written declared that God created mankind (Gen. 5:1). The God who made us surely intended us for a purpose. It is God who gives the spirit of life to a human soul. There can be no conception if He does not will it. So each of us were born on purpose. That means He knows you, cares about you, has a plan for you. And God is now prolonging the length of the "dash" between our birth and death dates for a purpose. Have you found it? Let me tell you about one of those I think found it. Della Jordan, one of my first impressions of a godly woman, was one of those "shouting Methodists" in the 1930's that kept the Wesleyan-Holiness-Pentecostal revival fervor going. She often invited different families home to Sunday dinner following Third Sunday meetings at Mount Pleasant. She served a gracious meal with no hidden agenda except to be a godly influence. She spoke often of the Lord to those around her table. She only spoke well of any members of the community. Every time my family came to her home, she would say, "You have blessed me by coming." A spinster, she lived only to serve the community. She visited homes to help care for the sick. When someone died, she would go to the home and assist with the washing and preparation of the body for burial. There were many such lives represented in those headstone inscriptions in the Mount Pleasant cemetery.

You do not have to become famous in order to fulfill the purpose of your own "dash." You just have to know Christ as your Savior and consciously live to serve Him. Then He will be in you, "working in you both to will and to do of His good pleasure" (Phil. 2:13b). That's what the "dash" is for. Pray that your life will be a dash filled with the presence of Jesus. And that no one will wonder for what purpose was the dash between birth and death. I trust God that my own dash is taking on more meaning as He continues to spare and extend my life. I'm here on purpose. His purpose!

SOMEONE TO TAKE YOUR HAND

"For I the LORD thy God will hold thy right hand, saying unto thee, Fear not; I will help thee." Isaiah 41:13

"There will be moments when all you can do to help someone is to just be there with them. It's reciprocal. There will also be moments when all someone else can do is to just be with you."

I recall a time in the early 1960's when I was serving as pastor of Glendale Baptist Church in Greenville, Mississippi. One of our church members, a Mr. Franklin, was critically ill in the hospital. I visited in his room when he had just been told he had only a few hours left. I asked him what I could do to help. He asked me if I would please just stay with him, and of course I did.

His wife and other family members came, and he tried to tell them he was dying. They rebuked him, saying, "Now don't talk like that! You're going to be all right. You're not going to die!" So, he couldn't say things he really wanted to say to his family. He did try, however. He asked them to please ask his brother to forgive him for something that he had done years earlier. He wanted to send word to several others that he forgave them and didn't have any hard feelings. He told his wife he loved her. He sent word to his children that he loved them.

Finally, the family was asked to leave. But because Mr. Franklin desired it, the doctor permitted me to stay until the end. He was quite lucid. Even when the nurse could not find the IV stand five minutes before he passed, he was able to tell her that she would find it behind the door. He asked me to pray and I took his hand and did so. We committed his soul into the hands of God. After the prayer I continued to hold his hand and after a moment he said, "I'm afraid. Please don't leave me." I promised I'd stay. I said, "I'll still be holding this hand when Jesus takes you by the other hand. When you feel His hand, you can squeeze mine and I'll know to let you go."

It was a wonderful moment when Mr. Franklin smiled and squeezed my hand. There was such great peace in the room that the doctor commented about it. I felt the Lord there. And I knew that someone else was now holding Mr. Franklin's hand. I let go as he breathed out his last breath. What about you? Do you know for sure you will have someone to take your hand on the other side? Here is God's promise: "For I the Lord thy God will hold thy right hand, saying unto thee, Fear not; I will help thee" (Isaiah 41:13). The last and greatest enemy we will face in this world is physical death. Everything else you will ever face is a far lesser terror. When you have peace about dying, you will have faith and fortitude for facing anything that the enemy brings against you before then. Going through life having God hold your hand! Seek *that* assurance today.

FACING TROUBLES HEAD-ON

"And now, behold, I go bound in the spirit unto Jerusalem, not knowing the things that shall befall me there: Save that the Holy Ghost witnesseth in every city, saying that bonds and afflictions abide me. But none of these things move me, neither count I my life dear unto myself, so that I might finish my course with joy, and the ministry, which I have received of the Lord Jesus, to testify the gospel of the grace of God." Acts 20:22-24

"Some troubles must be directly faced in order to get on with the rest of your life."

This scripture comes from near the end of the third missionary journey. Paul was meeting for the last time with the Ephesian elders. He was on his way to Jerusalem, in spite of the fact that he knew that imprisonment and afflictions awaited him there. But the God-appointed path of ministry that would take him to Rome lay directly through the troubles at Jerusalem. He would not allow the fear of trouble to cause him to leave the appointed course. When I was an undergraduate at Clarke Memorial College in Mississippi, the science class had a field trip to the Gulf of Mexico. There we boarded a fishing trawler and went several miles offshore to put down a net. We wanted to catch specimens for the science lab. During the day, the captain began to study the sky nervously. When a dark line of clouds began to loom on the horizon and the waves began to increase, he called me to the wheel.

"Have you ever steered a ship in a storm?" he asked. I said, "No." I didn't want to add that I had never steered a ship at all. "Well," he said, "You're the biggest guy here, and I'm going to need someone with muscle. That squall is about to hit. I have to go to the stern and operate the winch motor to get the net up. Here's what I want you to do: Hold this compass heading. That will keep the bow directly into the waves. Whatever you do – don't try to dodge a wave. That will turn us sideways and we'll capsize. Got that?" I got that. Especially the part about capsizing! In a few moments I was staring into waves higher than a house. As the ship rose and nosed down into a trough, it seemed I was looking overhead at the oncoming wave. It was the hardest thing to make the ship face those crashing waves, but it was the only way to keep from sinking. And eventually the captain returned and took over. We got through the storm.

There are things in life you wish you could avoid. But you can't. In fact, they'll do even more damage if you try to avoid them. They *must* be faced head-on. Sometimes, it's just doing the right thing about debt, employment, or bringing order to your household. Sometimes it is facing the consequences of poor decision making. Sometimes it is facing opposition when you answer the call to the ministry. The path to a successful ministry lies through many troubles that you must face head-on. Are you thinking of something you've been trying to avoid, but it just won't go away? Instead of dreading it, why not think about how much better your life will be once this thing is settled. You have to get past it so that you can get on with the rest of your life. So, make today the first day of an intentional project to face it and get through with it. Deal with it and get past it!

WHEN A GOOD JOB ISN'T GOOD ENOUGH

"But seek ye first the kingdom of God, and his righteousness; and all these things shall be added unto you." Matthew 6:33

"There are times in the Kingdom of God when a good thing becomes the enemy of the best thing."

Jesus tells us that we are to seek, before all else, to find our proper place in the Kingdom of God. "First" here in the Scripture is "proton" in Greek and means both first in sense of timing and first in sense of what is best. The Kingdom of God is our first consideration, and it is our first priority. For many years I have taught the principle that "the good can be the enemy of the best." That is when we let doing a good thing prevent us from doing the best thing in the sight of God. The word "kingdom" is from the Greek "basileia." That is a word which refers to authority or rulership. We are bound by this command of our Lord to always see that His plan overrides all other plans. We may have a good plan, but if it's not the plan of God, it becomes evil. It is evil because it replaces the one best thing God intended for you at that time.

Let me share an example of what I mean. In the year 1959 I was newly married and needed a job. I was still preaching part-time and had to supplement my income. Seeking help from an employment firm, I found favor with the manager of the firm, Henry Maxwell. Instead of getting me a job with another company, he hired me himself. He thought I would do well as a job counselor. The firm, located in Jackson, Mississippi, was then known as Brown's Employment Agency. All went well for the first six months. I earned several commissions per week, and learned the business quickly. But Mr. Maxwell decided to open his own agency, in competition with Brown's. Being prevented by law from working as a competitor, Mr. Maxwell hired me to be the manager of his new firm. He would provide the funding to start the company and I would manage it for the first six months. We leased space on the third floor of a prestigious high-rise office building in downtown Jackson. I chose the name, "Jobs, Inc." I hired several job counselors, and we started advertising.

Business poured in. I was earning a base salary plus an override commission on all the placement earnings of the job counselors. It amounted to what was an incredibly good income in 1959: more than $700 per week. It did not at first seem to conflict with my call to the preaching ministry. I could still use my weekends for preaching engagements. But after about three months I came face to face with one of those watershed life decisions. A church invited me to preach a week-long revival meeting later in the year. I thought that since I had worked such long hours getting the business started for Mr. Maxwell, that he would be sympathetic to my need to take a week off from work. After all, the revival engagement was still two months away, and by then I would surely have earned five days of vacation. But the boss was adamant that I could not have the week off. He said something that startled me: "You need to decide between this job and preaching." I didn't want to have to make that choice. But he was right. With that kind of income, I had begun thinking that maybe I could just be a faithful church member, tithe, and support the ministry as a layperson. But God reminded me of my life calling, and the promises I made to Him when He saved me and called me to the Gospel ministry. I had been called to preach, and my wife Jackie had been called to be a preacher's wife even before we met. The next day I told Henry Maxwell that I would be giving up the job. He was shocked. He really didn't expect that to be my decision.

I went on to preach the revival meeting. So far as I could observe, the results were not earthshaking. The offering that the church gave me wasn't either. And we did struggle financially for several months, until I was called to pastor another church. But I look back upon my decision to leave Jobs, Inc. as a landmark decision in my life. I had almost let something good rob me of the best that God had for me. But I made the right choice, and I have never been sorry. For over 45 years since then, my wife and I have seen God use us – planting churches, saving souls, changing lives. Through all those years, He has been faithful to supply every true need. In fact, we live in the abundance of God's blessings. Are you on the edge of a watershed decision like that? Do you know some best thing that you really ought to do, but you're afraid to let go and give up some present good thing? May God grant you the wisdom to choose rightly; and may He give you the grace to trust Him. Life is too short for us to squander our years on second-best things. Go for the best and let God do the rest!

A CRACKED RIB MIGHT BE A MESSAGE FROM GOD

""But the angel of the LORD stood in a path of the vineyards, a wall being on this side, and a wall on that side. And when the ass saw the angel of the LORD, she thrust herself unto the wall, and crushed Balaam's foot against the wall: and he smote her again." Numbers 22:24-25

"Sometimes when you have trouble going forward, you should check to see if that is really the right direction."

One of the ways God preserves us from a big trouble is to give us a small trouble. Balaam did not have as much spiritual discernment as did his donkey. The only way God could get his attention was to allow the donkey to crush his foot. Paul in the Book of Acts had proper discernment. When he wanted to preach in Asia, he was forbidden by the Holy Spirit. Then he tried to go to Bithynia, and the Holy Spirit also hindered that, because neither of these directions was right. Sometimes when you have trouble going forward, you should check to see if that is really the right direction. Paul found out that the right direction for him at that time was toward Macedonia. Paul is a good example of one who could tell when he was on a wrong path. Balaam could only know it when his foot was crushed. We could save ourselves a lot of trouble by paying more attention to the Holy Spirit.

In 1982, I was visiting a ministry friend named John Kimlingen in rural Connecticut when I learned this lesson the hard way. John headed what was called "Burning Bush Ministries." We were on his farm where about a dozen teenage boys and girls were going through rehabilitation. Most of them had been rescued from the drug culture. In a wholesome environment of farm life and Bible study, they were all doing well. But John was not. He had one kidney that had lost all function, and only about 10% use of the other remained. He had dialysis twice a week in his own fully equipped dialysis room at home. One day I sat with him during the process. As the nurse was unhooking tubes from his body, John said, "Let's go horseback riding." The nurse reminded him that was not on his list of permitted activities. But John was adamant. He always enjoyed the horses, and he was missing the rides.

So two of the youth, John and I made a foursome of riders and set out carefully across an old cornfield. John urged his horse to a gallop, and we all had to do the same to keep up. As we were flying down the cornfield, my saddle slipped and I fell from the horse. A sharp pain in my ribs and in my shoulder told me I had cracked or broken something. But when John came riding back to check on me, I laughed it off and said I was okay. How I wish today that I had told the whole truth then. We would have turned around and gone back to the farm. But the others were really enjoying the ride, so I remounted tenderly and we rode on. Soon we crossed a shallow, stony stream. As John's horse started up the opposite bank, he slipped and fell backwards. John fell against a log in the stream, and struck it with his back squarely in the spot where his one kidney was located. He was in no shape to ride, but we were in a remote area.

We put him back on the horse and I led his horse on foot through the woods to the nearest farm house. From there we finally got him to a hospital. John never fully recovered. About six weeks later, he passed away. When I got home from that trip, x-rays showed that I had a cracked collar bone and three cracked ribs. I am convinced that those cracked ribs were warnings from God that we should have turned back. Lessons learned at so great a price are never forgotten. Are you trying to do the wrong thing, or the right thing at the wrong time? God loves you, and He surely will give you some warning signs. But the more stubborn you are, the more it will cost you. Stop and think and pray. It may save you a crushed foot or some cracked ribs!

STAY WITH THE PROCESS

"And thou shalt remember all the way which the Lord thy God led thee these forty years in the wilderness, to humble thee, and to prove thee, to know what was in thine heart, whether thou wouldest keep his commandments, or no. And he humbled thee, and suffered thee to hunger, and fed thee with manna, which thou knewest not, neither did thy fathers know; that he might make thee know that man doth not live be bread only, but by every word that pro-ceedeth out of the mouth of the LORD doth man live." Deuteronomy 8: 2-3

"God has brought you through a process, and you must allow that process to continue."

The Israelites had just finished 40 years of wilderness wan-dering. God was reminding them through Moses what it had cost to just get to the banks of the Jordan. They had been put through a time of testing. God had led them a certain way through the wilderness for all that time. It was a necessary learning process. The process helped them learn to live by the word of God.

A lady heard me teach and came up afterward and said she wanted my "mantle." She wanted to have what I had, a gifting and an anointing to teach the Word of God. She was referring to Elijah leaving his mantle to Elisha, and to Elisha starting out on the same kind of ministry. It was a nice thought, but she and I both knew it wouldn't happen like that. Even Elisha had to walk for years in the shadow of Elijah and go through all the testings and lessons and hardships that Elijah did.

Here is what made me who I am as a teacher. I have gone through a process of 45 years in ministry: Pioneering churches, preaching to spiritually calloused people, watching parents ignore God and pass the attitude on to their children, living on no salary or small salary. Going through heartbreak after heartbreak when my efforts in the ministry met with failure. Going through hardships. Raising a family. Years of pain and almost dying of Lupus. Going through grief over loss of loved ones. Losing and regaining the victory dozens of times. Fighting the Devil in Haiti, Yucatan, Jamaica, Columbia and dozens of other countries. Trying to mentor young ministers. Watching God make examples out of other preachers when they got proud and worldly. Growing old. The process involved all of that, and more!

So, nobody in their right mind would want to go through what I have gone through to get where I am. But God does have a process for every person. The principles of that process are easy enough to see in this chapter. First, The Process: humility and testing, verse 2-3; Secondly, The Result: live spiritually, verse 3; Thirdly, The Goals: note the three verbs in verse 6. Here's some advice: Don't fight this process. Don't get to the place that you cry out, "I don't need this!" Don't get to the point of verses 11 and 17. The high cost of doing so is in verse 19.

Don't set up a process of your own making. You could have avoided a lot of the trouble you have gone through – that you brought upon yourself. Just be where God wants you; do what God wants – and the process will happen. Embrace the process. Thank God for it. See Him as being fully in charge of your life! Think about how many different things had to happen to get you to this college! You also, dear reader, can reflect on all the different things that had to happen to bring you to this moment in which you read this and absorb this wonderful truth! It has been an amazing process – one that only God could arrange.

That's Romans 8:28 in action! There in Romans, Paul by the Holy Spirit reveals to us a great life principle. Your life will turn out better for having gone through all the hard things as well as the easy things. It will be even better because you faced some evil things as well as all the good things. Times of darkness as well as times of light; times of turmoil as well as times of peace; times of togetherness as well as times of loneliness are all important ingredients that God can use. Really, when you understand this, you will see the greatness of Father God. He is able to take all things and make you better through them. Accept God's love, His power, and His wisdom, and embrace His process for you!

WHAT DO YOU REALLY, REALLY WANT IN LIFE?

"And Moses said unto the Lord, See, thou sayest unto me, Bring up this people: and thou hast not let me know whom thou wilt send with me. Yet thou has said, I know thee by name, and thou hast also found grace in my sight. Now therefore, I pray thee, if I have found grace in thy sight, show me now thy way, that I may know thee, that I may find grace in thy sight: and consider that this nation is thy people. ...And he said unto him, If thy presence go not with me, carry us not up hence. ...And he said, I beseech thee, show me thy glory. Exodus 33:12-13; 33:15; 33:18

"There are three great desires that God promises to fulfill."

We have all heard funny stories that start with someone finding a bottle and a genie pops out and says you can have just three wishes, but you can have anything you wish for. Well, *that* won't ever happen! But *God* says He will give us the desires of our heart.

In Psalm 37:4, God says, "Delight thyself also in the Lord; and he shall give thee the desires of thine heart." That's a divine promise. But here's the way it works. The world, the flesh, and the devil have left their mark on your natural heart. But God by His Spirit has been quietly developing good and righteous desires in you also. So at times you are startled to realize that something you always thought you wanted is no longer appealing. And you are surprised at yourself when you have a desire that only God can place in your heart.

I remember when I about 32 years old, and was in New Orleans Seminary hearing someone talk about going to the land of the Bible. He spoke about actually seeing some of the places mentioned in Scripture. I remember thinking, I'd really, really like to do that. It was a brand new thought, because previously I was never interested at all in going to Israel. But of course I was on a small salary supporting a family, and I had neither funds nor time to go.

Then I graduated and I was hired at the same Seminary to serve as Public Relations Director. Not long after that I heard about an archaeological tour organized by our new Archaeology professor. Students would get academic credit for participating in a dig in Israel, and they would be there six weeks. They would get to go on tours of holy sites every weekend. I really, really wanted to go – but I had a job and a family.

One morning, the seminary president called me in his office and said, "I want you to think about something. Our Archeology professor has resigned at the last minute. We already have this joint dig with Tel Aviv University organized, and students have paid their money. I need you to go and serve as business manager and leader of the group. If we pay your way and continue your salary while you are gone, would you like to go? Pray about it and get back to me.

Well, it so happened that at that time in my life, I felt like I was caught up with my praying, but I did go home and ask my wife. She was supportive and said she and the babies could manage, and might even get to make a couple of trips back to her home in Jackson, Mississippi. So I wound up going on an expense paid trip to Israel – still earning my salary, and having the experience of a lifetime! It changed me, and I have since led over 30 tours to Israel, and wound up working a while as a consulate director for the International Christian Embassy in Israel.

Know what? I left New Orleans and went 8,000 miles a way, and yet the same Jesus I knew here in my daily walk went with me and was beside me at every biblical site, helping me to understand more about it than I ever did before. It was a great spiritual adventure for me. My way there was made by Him, His presence was with me, and He showed more of His glory. Now the world, the flesh, the Devil didn't want me to go to Israel. Only God could have put that desire in me. And when I least expected it, He brought it to fulfillment. So here was a great lesson in my life.

Have you ever just taken the time to stop and think about your life and the big pictures in it? At your funeral, what will they say you have achieved in life? Regardless of what you are caught up in, or feel you have to do – what do you really, really want in life? We are reading the prayer of Moses that expressed his utmost desires. See how his prayer contrasts with our usual requests! It's not about getting bills paid, or getting a car, or a house. It's not even about getting healed or delivered.

Here's what we should be praying for: First, for God's Way,

v. 13. We have to start with that. Otherwise we will go down some wrong paths. Secondly, we must have God's Presence, v. 15. How can you be happy if you don't have that? There is a God-shaped vacuum in your heart that only he can fill. You lose the sense of His presence when you sin. He's there, but your heart has closed him out. Pray for your thoughts to become clean enough and your heart pure enough, that you go all day in His presence. Thirdly, we need to see God's Glory, v. 18. How many people have settled for living their whole life without ever knowing it? The worst mistake you can make is thinking you have arrived spiritually when you have never seen God's glory in your life. The world is filled with spiritual pygmies who think they are spiritual giants. They have never had a visitation from God in which they had to fall down because they could not stand, and in which God showed them how awesome He is.

You start with the Way. That is your first assignment. Learn to see and follow God's road markers. Then you want God to go with you – you want His presence. Then you want to see the One who is walking with you – you want to see the glory of God: Way, Presence, Glory. What do you really, really want? That's what you should be talking to God about. You believe God's way includes this college. Well, while you are here, seek His presence and His glory!

SETTING OFF DIVINE CHAIN REACTIONS

"In all thy ways acknowledge him, and he shall direct thy paths." Proverbs 3:6

"Few have discovered the secret of being in the right place and the right time in the plan of God, but it can set off amazing chain reactions of God's providence."

The root word here for "acknowledge" is *yada'* which is a key word in the Old Testament. It is used 944 times and has a variety of connotations regarding knowledge. In this context it means to have knowledge of God's will and to make it known. Then, God promises here to direct your paths. Some of life's choices are easy. Suppose you have a job that does not suit your lifestyle as a believer. You want to change jobs, but you like the pay and you're not sure where to go next. So you don't do anything. Then you get laid off. Now you can easily decide to get another job.

But some of life's choices are hard. I remember a church that my wife and I planted in Greenville, Mississippi. The congregation grew steadily and a new building was built on new property. At the end of three years we had a strong church and the pastor's salary was the most generous I had ever received. Yet there was a growing conviction that God wanted me to move to New Orleans to study in a seminary there. I had put my post graduate studies on hold for the three years that we were pioneering the new church. Finally, on a Sunday morning when the sanctuary was packed and eleven souls had responded to a salvation invitation, I announced my resignation. I didn't resign because of trouble in the church, nor because of need for more income. There was no logical reason. We loved those people, and they loved us. Our second child was born while we were there. We had many wonderful memories. It was a hard decision, but after much prayer, We knew it was what God wanted. That decision set off a chain reaction of divinely appointed events. First, while in New Orleans, I met a Gideon who was thrilled to learn that I had been saved in jail while reading a Gideon placed New Testament. He persuaded the program committee of the New Orleans Gideons' annual banquet to invite me as a speaker. That led to an invitation to speak at the International Gideon convention in Detroit, and to my story being printed in a Gideon book called *Pastors All*. That led to numerous contacts with Gideons all over the country, often leading to evangelistic opportunities.

Second, while in New Orleans, my wife and I were invited to help a small group of three families to help plant a church in a new neighborhood next to the Michoud Space Center. That church grew and even helped ordain and send out other ministers in the brief time I remained as pastor. On Sunday nights the entire church would go to the French Quarter to pass out tracts and witness. It remains a strongly evangelistic church today. Third the decision to go to New Orleans allowed me to meet the famous Chaplain of Bourbon Street,

Bob Harrington. He helped me develop a new boldness in my personal witness. He introduced me to the ministry of visiting bars for Christ. I learned I could go inside, ask the manager for 5 minutes to preach the Gospel, and in most cases get permission! Fourth, because of that decision made back in Greenville, Mississippi, my leadership skills were greatly enhanced. I began by campaigning to be the seminary's student body newsletter editor. We took the newsletter, called the *Canon*, to a new level. Then I campaigned for the position of student government president and won. My success at that post led to employment in the seminary administration when I graduated. I became director of public relations, and then director of development.

Fifthly, the decision led me to eventually to Israel. the Seminary sent me on an expense paid archaeological expedition to Israel, where I served as business manager of a dig at Beersheeba. That summer God forged in my heart a love for the land of Israel. I eventually served as a consulate director for the International Christian Embassy in Jerusalem; to working with the Jewish community in Atlanta; and to conducting Bless Israel rallies in churches throughout the southeast. Over the years I led over 30 tour groups to Israel. I wonder how different my life would be if I had not made that decision to leave the church in Greenville to go to seminary.

Finally, the decision caused me to be in the right place and the right time for my next assignment. A Florida church contacted the Seminary for help finding a new pastor. God spoke to me and told me to offer myself. Again, it was one of those hard decisions. Financially, my family and I were better off where we were. Also, because of my position in the Seminary administration, I was beginning to be recognized in the Southern Baptist Convention. But after prayer, we decided to go to Milton Florida. In the next three years we enjoyed tremendous blessing. The church allowed me to lead them into experimental ministry models, and there we pioneered the "task group" concept and a bus ministry. We baptized every Wednesday night for three years and became known as the "Church Aflame." Pastors and staff from other churches came to observe. The move from New Orleans was God's plan, but it would have never happened if we had never made the decision to move to New Orleans!

Perhaps you have just made such a decision. You have decided to do something you don't quite understand yourself. Family and friends don't know what to make of it. But you feel in your heart that God led you. Or, maybe you face such a decision now. Just pray and ask God to clear your spiritual mind of all other options. Seek the peace of settling on a course of action you know will please God. Just do the right thing! That will take you down a path to lifelong blessing – it will be your ticket to the greatest show on earth! Just do what God wants right now, and He will show himself in your life in a spectacular, amazing chain of events.

THANK AND PRAISE GOD FOR
IT BEFORE IT HAPPENS

"And it came to pass at the seventh time, when the priests blew with the trumpets, Joshua said unto the people, Shout; for the LORD hath given you the city." Joshua 6:16

"Sometimes the blessing won't come until you praise God before it happens. You can do this because of true faith. To you it is as good as done."

A careful reading of this story reveals that before the wall fell, the army was required to shout because, as the verse says, "...the Lord hath given you the city." It was an accomplished fact, though there was no outward sign that it was so! Jesus did something like that at the grave of Lazarus. He said, "...Father, I thank thee that thou hast heard me." And then he shouted with "... a loud voice, Lazarus, come forth." Thanks and praises are in order even before something happens – because you know God has heard you. A line from a praise chorus says, "When the praises go up, the blessings come down." It is in order to praise God – at all times. But if you are claiming some promise of God, you should act like you believe it. Start giving God the glory. Any fool can thank God after something has turned out all right, but it takes faith to thank him in advance! A day or so after the walls fell at Jericho, Joshua lost a battle at Ai. God told him there was sin in the camp. Then when Joshua dealt with it, God told Joshua to try again at Ai. God said, "...arise, and go up to Ai: see, I have given into thy hand the king of Ai, and his people, and his city, and his land." Again, here is a complete victory spoken of in the past tense – even before it happened!

Once I was looking for a small farm where I could relocate my family during a time of low income. Weekend after weekend, we drove out of town and searched and followed up on ads. Everything was more than we could afford. Disappointed, I decided to give up on the project. Then, sometime later I was on an errand and drove past a small hand lettered sign on a tree. For some reason I took down the number and called the lady who owned the land. She wanted me to meet her where I saw the sign, and she would show me the property. It was heavily wooded and overgrown with briars and vines, but the price sounded reasonable, so I drove back out to the place. I got there a few minutes early. When I stepped out of my car, I stepped into a small bag of household trash that someone had thrown out. A portion of the Bible was in it. As I bent over, I read these words from Genesis 13:17: "Arise, walk through the land in the length of it and in the breadth of it; for I will give it unto thee."

The owner arrived. I looked over the property with her. I was thinking, "Lord, even if I buy this land, I won't have any money left to develop it. I will need to dig a well and build a driveway. Then I'll have to get a house built." But something happened in my heart. I thought about the promise in the Scripture. Then I just felt to go ahead and thank God for the whole thing! I was walking through the woods on the property – and just thanking God. As I did so, I stumbled over a well curb hidden in the leaves. No need to dig a well. I found an old driveway. No need to hire a bulldozer contractor. This had once been a home site. I had the well cleaned out, and moved a modular house into place, and we started homesteading and clearing land for pastures, a garden and a vineyard.

For the next seventeen years my family and I enjoyed the beauty and serenity of that farm. I was surrounded by forest and had to maintain a half-mile driveway through the woods to the highway. But it was as secluded as any mountain retreat. Friends who came to visit almost always remarked about how beautiful and peaceful our place was. My children grew up there in that haven of peace. We enjoyed having animals and space to wander around on quiet walks. It was such a blessing! But before it happened, I began to believe I had it. And I started thanking the Lord! I shudder at the thought of all that might not have happened had I continued to doubt.

Maybe I am talking to someone here who has adopted a "wait and see" attitude about whether a certain blessing is going to come to you. Today you are being reminded to go ahead and start praising God for it. You already know enough to praise about! All things are working together for good. No good thing is being withheld from you. God says so in His word. Start believing you have all you need. And then start thanking Him for giving you the desires of your heart.

RIGHTEOUS SERENDIPITY

"The steps of a good man are ordered by the LORD: and he delighteth in his way. Psalms 37:23

"When it's the right thing to do and you do it, unexpected blessings will overtake you. I call that righteous serendipity."

After leading many tour groups to Israel, I had a hunger to back go alone. I always was so occupied in providing leadership and teaching for the groups that I had no personal time with the Lord at the various holy sites. I did not mention this desire to anyone other than my wife. Of course I knew I could never afford to go on my own. I always went with groups because the commissions I received from the travel company paid my way. But in my heart I longed to just travel without a group and make a personal pilgrimage to the Holy Land.

During the time I worked for the International Christian Embassy, I served here in Atlanta as consulate director. We worked as a link between pro-Israel churches and the Atlanta Jewish civic community. On one occasion the JNF (Jewish National Fund) was sponsoring a "10K" march through North Atlanta to raise funds for the town of Yemen in Israel. My wife and I decided that as Christians we ought to get in the march and show our support. Our pastor and his wife agreed to march with us. Holding a large banner I had ordered, the four of us Christians took our place that morning and began to march with the Jews up Peachtree Street. At a certain intersection where the march took a turn off Peachtree, some television news teams were set up to cover the event. It so happened that our banner attracted their attention and this was not only shown on the evening news, but a photo was also printed in the morning issue of the *Atlanta Journal & Constitution* paper. The caption mistakenly identified the long line of Jewish people behind our banner as hundreds of Christians out marching with Jews.

I called the newspaper the next day, and the march organizers as well, to correct the story. But the Jewish leaders were very happy for the attention we had gotten. Regardless of the disproportionate attention we had received, it helped convey the message of Christian friendship and support. Funds raised by the march were going to provide a new park and playground equipment for the little town of Yemen near the Lud Airport. I was happy that we had a small part in that. Then something wonderful happened! The JNF wanted to honor me with a visit to the town of Yemen in Israel. The Israeli Consulate arranged for a free trip on El Al airlines.

Still in shock, I flew first class and was greeted graciously in the town by the mayor and community leaders. They had arranged a folk festival for my entertainment. Then I was privileged to travel with an Israeli army captain as escort to all the holy sites I wanted to visit. It was a dream come true. The desire of my heart to had been to visit each place as a pilgrim and to have time alone there with God. On that one trip, everything came to fulfillment! Not only that, but I went horseback riding in Galilee, went on a camera safari in a game reserve, and visited in the homes of both Arab and Jewish leaders. That trip was one of the high points of my life!

I have learned something I would like to pass on to you. Doing the right thing will result in your being in the right place at the right time for God to bestow upon you the desires of your heart. That is righteous serendipity. You stumble into blessings exceeding abundantly above all that you ask or think. My counsel to you is that you should put yourself in position for the desires of your heart to be fulfilled. But you position yourself not by trying to get your desires fulfilled, but simply doing the right thing at the moment. Do the right thing, one day at a time. Let your steps be ordered by the Lord. And one day, those steps will lead to some delightful surprise!

DON'T TRY TO PICK APPLES OFF A DEAD TREE

"But in whatsoever city ye enter, and they receive you not, go your ways out into the streets of the same, and say, Even the very dust of your city, which cleaveth on us, we do wipe off against you: notwithstanding be ye sure of this, that the kingdom of God is come nigh to you." Luke 10:10-11

"There will be times when you have to move on. Why waste time with people who are not open to your message, while thousands in another place hungrily await your arrival?"

Jesus here is telling his disciples that there are times to

move on. If your ministry has been rejected, do not continue to waste your time in that place. It is like picking apples. You don't continue to expect apples on a dead tree. Some of you have spent a lot of time looking again and again for apples on a dead tree. If that is the case, I want to encourage you to look to another field of ministry. If you want to see things happen in God's kingdom, go where the tree is alive and capable of bearing fruit. If you really like seeing lots of people joyfully embrace the good news of Christ; if you long to see crowds of people being baptized in the Holy Spirit – you need to move on from where you are.

In 1972, I agreed to come and serve as pastor of a certain Baptist church in Decatur, Georgia. Prior to the decision to do so, I met several times with the pulpit committee. The members of this committee all testified to a mighty move of God in their own lives. Several of them had received the baptism of the Holy Spirit. They told me that not only themselves, but many members of the congregation were openly seeking the baptism of the Holy Spirit. They sought me out because they knew that I was a Spirit-baptized Baptist pastor who could come and lead the church further on in renewal.

Within five months, the church grew to the maximum capacity of the building. Chairs had to be placed up every aisle every Sunday. The worship style was fully charismatic. Miraculous healings were happening during altar time. Souls were being saved in every service. Something else was happening: many were beginning to speak in tongues, though not in the worship service. Most of the congregation was happy.

But not all. The board of deacons felt that the church was becoming too Pentecostal. They also felt that their leadership was being undermined. So, an unofficial phone tree was put into action. Every inactive and active member of the church was asked to be present in a Wednesday night business meeting.

In that meeting, swelled to five times the normal attendance, the church voted to fire me. In the dicussion someone pointed out that the manifestations of the Spirit we were experiencing were in the Bible. But one of the deacons countered with the statement, "It may be in the Bible, but it's not what Baptists believe." And that was that. My wife and I drove home in stunned silence. We had never been dismissed from a church before. There were no savings to fall back on. What would we do?

A group of friends were waiting at our home that night. We had prayer. Afterward, we all felt the peace of the Lord. Rather than feeling defeated, I felt released. God moved us on that week to start a dynamic church that was fully Charismatic, very evangelistic and that launched a great number of missionaries into global missions. During the start-up months, we had to be frugal, but God was faithful and we never got behind financially. The first church, however, went drastically down in attendance: from 1,000 to less than 200 within a month. They continued to struggle, and eventually relocated to a suburb further out of the city. There they also struggled financially, and finally sold their property and relocated again.

A few years after I had been voted out of the church in Decatur, the pastor of a Baptist Church in North Georgia read a copy of my book, *The Shepherd's Touch*. This book about the baptism of the Holy Spirit had resonated in his spirit. He was persuaded that I must come to his church and help lead them in a week of revival. I arranged a time to come to his church to see what the Lord would do. The second night, miracles began to happen. A deacon was healed of a foot injury. Another was healed of severe back pain. A lady had a lump disappear. The pastor was ecstatic. But not everyone shared his joy. Two of the wealthiest deacons met with him after the second service and delivered an ultimatum. Either I had to leave, or they would. The pastor came later than evening to my hotel room to tell me that he had decided to stop the meetings. I could tell his heart was heavy. I pressed him to honestly say whether he thought that the miracles were the work of God. He said he knew they were. Also, that what I was teaching was right. But, nevertheless, he felt that we should not continue.

I then told him essentially what Jesus said in Luke 10:10-11. My conscience was clear. I left and went back to the work I had interrupted to come to that engagement. And God continued to bless and use me. God has opened for me a ministry that reaches across the world. I can preach to thousands of hungry souls and see miracles in every meeting. To my knowledge, that church has since stuck to its traditions and has never experienced revival.

Perhaps you share my desire to be where I can do the most

good. You want be where people respond to your message – where your time is not being wasted. Take a long look at the leadership structure where you are. Is that going to be a hindrance? Observe the lifestyles and interests of the people. Do they show any real openness to spiritual change? You may need to seek God's guidance and follow it to a new place of service. Don't waste your precious time on people who are not open. Stop looking for apples on dead trees.

" THE DARK VALLEY "

"Yea, though I walk through the valley of the shadow of death, I will fear no evil: for thou art with me; thy rod and thy staff they comfort me." Psalm 23:4

"There is an experience ahead for you and every soul when you will be in the valley of death – only hours or minutes away from eternity. All that will matter then is that the Lord is with you."

David, the sweet psalmist of Israel, was a gifted song writer that could paint pictures with words. He was an outdoorsman, a shepherd. He had often been in the mountains late in the day. He had seen the shadows gather quickly and noticed how dark the valleys became when the time was near sunset. He used that picture to speak of the time when he would walk through the valley of death at the sunset of his life. He had no fear because he knew the Lord would always be with him.

Have you ever contemplated your own mortality? Many people are so afraid of even the thought of death that they will never make out a will nor leave any funeral instructions. We are told in the Bible that the last enemy that shall be destroyed is death. But we who have the Spirit of Christ already know the presence of the One who has conquered death. So death holds no sting for us. My wife and I have already prepaid our funeral expenses and purchased companion crypts. I sometimes drive by the site on Rose Avenue in Douglasville and stop by the mausoleum that has my name inscribed on it. It doesn't bother me at all – it's just part of the stewardship of life to make arrangements for what your death would otherwise cost your family.

You see, I've already been in the dark valley. Over twenty years ago I was at the point of death in Cottonwood Clinic near Dothan, Alabama. The inflammation caused by Lupus had traveled up my spinal column into my brain and swollen it. I was not expected to live. As my brain began to lose its functions, I found myself in a trance. I was somewhere in the North Georgia Mountains where I used to go backpacking with my son. The sun was low and the mountains were high. I was down in a very dark valley floor, hearing a gurgling mountain stream nearby in the darkness. I sensed the presence of the Lord Jesus beside me. He spoke: "You don't know whether I will take you across that stream or if we will just walk together a while just on this side. But whatever happens, will you be equally pleased?" I remember hearing my soul say, "Oh! Yes, Lord."

The next morning I awakened with a clear mind and the absence of pain. For the first time in weeks I was able to walk. Jesus had walked with me in the dark valley. And he helped me realize that there was no fear there. Then he healed me and gave me all this extra time! That was a defining moment for me. First, it changed all my priorities. Secondly, the experience did something else for me of which I was unaware until the next time I came close to death. It permanently relieved me of my fear of dying. About 20 years later, I had a heart attack. During two occasions in the hospital, the medical team performed sensitive operations. I was fully conscious, talking with the surgeon as he worked. We spoke about his own recent conversion. When he completed a difficult step far more easily than expected, we both acknowledged that the Lord had helped him. I noticed something about myself as I lay on the operating table. There was not the slightest fear of dying. Thirdly, being in the dark valley has removed my fear of everything else. When you're equally ready to go and ready to stay, you can face everything without fear. Now, all that thrills my soul is Jesus. And all I'll need in that future hour that I will leave this life is the assurance of his precious presence.

A L O S T P E N N Y

"I know both how to be abased, and I know how to abound: every where and in all things I am instructed both to be full and to be hungry, both to abound and to suffer need." Philippians 4:12

"God arranges for each one of us to be tested in both poverty and plenty. I have been tested both ways."

Crossing the parking lot, I picked up a stray penny. Many others had walked on by it, thinking it was not worth bending over to retrieve it. As I picked it up, I said something to the person beside me like, "I always do this – I feel it's being a good steward." My friend said, "Yes, but how can you tithe a penny?" Actually, it's very easy. The penny is your firstfruits. According to the Bible, that's the portion that belongs to God – the first tenth. So when I find a penny, I know nine more are coming! When I get a dollar, I can either tithe like most people do, and give God back a dime – or I can tithe in faith and give Him the whole dollar back. I have learned to do that, unless otherwise instructed by the Lord. And most of the time, He lets me do it. He seems to enjoy the game as much as I do, and very soon, nine more dollars show up – dollars only He could have provided. Only when I get greedy and do it for the wrong motive will it not work out that way. If I do it just for the joy of bringing something to my Father, He always multiplies it.

I try to keep up with every bit of unexpected income and treat it as if it were that first penny. I put it into the thing closest to God's heart: world missions. The winning of souls for the kingdom. It's like investing in a bank CD that returns 100-fold. It just keeps on coming back. All the tithe of my regular income goes straight to my church – 10 percent and no strings. But I love unexpected income! It means I get to play the game.

Where did I come up with this odd way of tithing unexpected income? Well, I was homeless for a while. After getting saved in a New Orleans jail, I was released and had no where to go. I wandered about the downtown district, trying to find work. I had no money and no home. I stayed in the park at night for a while. Later I stayed at a Salvation Army shelter. I answered want ads, but my clothing had gotten shabby during my stay in jail. People were simply afraid to hire me. So, I was jobless and homeless in the city. Each day I would walk about with my head down, looking for stray coins. When I found a penny, I took heart. I looked and found nine more to go with it. Now I had a dime. When I had a few more pennies I had enough to go to White Castle and get a small hamburger and a glass of water. Sometimes I would find a dime. I was really happy then, because I worked on finding enough other coins to have a dollar. Then I could have a hamburger, a small root beer, and a slice of coconut crème pie!

Paul said, "I know how to be abased, and I know how to abound. Every where and in all things I am instructed both to be full and to be hungry, both to abound and to suffer need." Having been homeless taught me not to be wasteful. It taught me to be a good steward. It taught me to be faithful in small things – like picking up a penny! Therefore, I am grateful for having been homeless. When you learn how to do without, then you may be wise enough for God to let you have something to do with. When you learn how it feels to be hungry, God may let you know how it feels to be full. When you learn how to suffer need, God may then let you suffer abundance!

Let's pray that we will be found faithful in every little thing, so that we can move on to bigger things for the glory of God.

MY JEWISH ROOTS

"Even us, whom he hath called, not of the Jews only, but also of the Gentiles? As he saith also in Osee, I will call them my people, which were not my people; and her beloved, which was not beloved. And it shall come to pass, that in the place where it was said unto them, Ye are not my people; there shall they be called the children of the living God. Esaias also crieth concerning Israel, Though the number of the children of Israel be as the sand of the sea, a remnant shall be saved: For he will finish the work and cut it short in righteousness: because a short work will the Lord make upon the earth." "Brethren, my heart's desire and prayer to God for Israel is, that they might be saved." Romans 9: 24-28; 10:1

"In the family tree of those who are saved, Gentiles are the wild branches that are grafted in. The Gentile church will never be in good spiritual health until it understands and accepts the Hebrew Christianity known as Messianic Judaism. My own ministry has become more healthy since I have explored our Jewish roots."

Did you know that beginning with James the brother of John, the first 16 bishops of the Jerusalem church were all Jewish? Or that synagogues were the normal meeting places for churches during the first 90 years of Christianity? Of course you do know that our New Testament was written by Jews in a Jewish country and that it is all about Jesus who came into this world as a Jew in a Jewish culture. The point is that in our spiritual heritage, we are deeply indebted to the Jewish people. In Romans 9 we find that in the plan of God, both Jews and Gentiles will be saved. In Romans 10 we hear the heartbeat of God in verse 1. It is Paul's prayer that Jews will be saved. The wonderful thing about that is the tremendous number of Jews coming to their Messiah in recent years. There are hardly enough future Messianic rabbis in training to lead all the new congregations that are springing up.

Orthodox Jews in Atlanta have given me a Jewish name: it is pronounced Dag, meaning "fish." It fits since the fish is the symbol of a Christian. They gave me the name when I attended adult night classes sponsored by the Atlanta Jewish Federation Board of Education and learned to read, write and speak modern Hebrew. In my work with the International Christian Embassy in Jerusalem (ICEJ), I was privileged to serve as liaison with several Jewish agencies as well as the Israeli Consulate. I helped the JNF host a TV program called a "Tree-a-thon." I encouraged Christians in the audience to contribute to the work of planting trees in Israel. During that period I traveled across the Southeast US to large churches and conducted what we called "Bless Israel Rallies." I would take with me an Israeli representative of the JNF (known as a "Sheliach") and usually also some Israeli Consulate official. In the rallies these guests would be treated to some fast tempo Christian praise music with an Israeli beat and a Bible-based message on blessing Israel. They would be given a plaque of appreciation stating that that church had promised to pray for the peace of Jerusalem. The offering would go to planting trees in the land of Israel. In turn, they would present the church with an Israeli flag that had been flown over the Knesset.

On another occasion, I rented all the meeting facilities at the huge Atlanta Jewish Center on Peachtree Street to hold a one-day extravaganza we called an "Israel Festival." We featured an Israeli art show, Israel folk dancing, Israeli film festival, and a fully kosher Israeli breakfast. Many Jewish agencies such as the JNF, the Magen David Adom (literally, The "Red Shield of David" – like our Red Cross) and B'Nai B'Rith had display booths. Because of my help in encouraging support of Israel among Gentile churches, the Jewish officials began to introduce me as a "righteous Gentile!" We formed such a bond of trust that on one occasion the Anti-Defamation League of B'Nai B'Rith sent me out as a substitute luncheon speaker to a Rotary Club meeting!

A few years later, my wife Jackie and I had the wonderful privilege of being members of Congregation Beth Hallel in Roswell. Our long-time friends Robert and Dotti Solomon lead the congregation, whose name means "House of Praise." Robert is a converted Jew who now serves as rabbi to the thriving group – at least half of whom are also converted Jews. We were inspired and humbled by the wholehearted zeal with which Jewish converts were serving their Saviour. Although from the very first we were embraced with the love of Christ,

there were many terms and phrases unfamiliar to our vocabu-
lary. They referred to Jesus by His Hebrew name, Yeshua; or
His Hebrew title, Meshiach. They preferred to call the church
the "congregation." They referred to their meeting place as
a synagogue.

Moreover, the Messianic Jews use a liturgy of responsive
readings and chants that date back to the time of Christ. The
boy Jesus might well have said the very same words in the
synagogue services there in Nazareth. And they observe all
the traditional Jewish festivals and holy days – with added
meaning as Messianic believers (Christians). We gained new
appreciation for the spiritual and prophetic significance to
Christians of all the special days on the Jewish calendar. As
members of Beth Hallel we learned a new appreciation for the
Word of God, which was honored in every service with a ceremony in which the old scrolls were respectfully displayed in
the opening of the "ark" – a tall, ornate cabinet centrally located on the platform. During the time the ark was opened, the
people always stood in reverence. The weekly responsive
readings consistently drilled us on the holiness and the life of
God's Word. Then, at an appropriate time, we heard the
selected readings from the Old Testament (Torah) and from
the New Testament (B'rit Hadashah).

We learned too, the joy of praise. The congregation has a
great music ministry – even traveling groups who give con-
certs in various Gentile churches. The music has a distinctive
Israeli flavor and is very upbeat. Even guests at Beth Hallel
would find themselves clapping to the rhythm of praise songs.

Then there was the solemnity and reverence of worship songs that were directed from the heart to God himself. Who I am today has been partly shaped by my time spent as a member of the Beth Hallel fellowship.

The world in general and our country in particular is becoming more and more inhospitable to the Jewish people. Anti-Semitism, unchecked, will always lead to persecution of the Jews. But we must understand that the same evil spirit that hates the Jews also hates the Christians. After the Nazis came for the Jews in Germany, they came back for the Christians. Over 2 ½ million Christians were killed in the Holocaust along with the 6 million Jews who perished. We must realize that our roots in history and our future destiny in the plan of God have Gentiles and Jews inextricably bound together. We must take a stand. The first place to take a stand against anti-Semitism is to show support and solidarity with Messianic Judaism.

While you are doing that, you might find yourself gaining new insights. For example, as you attend Messianic services, you can see more clearly how the early Christians worshiped. You will be awed by the sound of the shofar, almost never heard in Gentile churches. In the liturgy of the ritual candle-lighting you will develop a deeper appreciation of the Sabbath, although you may continue to observe it on a different day. You will be touched by the spiritual symbolism of the prayer shawl (talit) and understand more fully what it means to be under the covering of God's laws. Going back to my Jewish roots helped shape my vision for inclusive intercultural ministry. I continue to have an excellent relationship with Beth Hallel. They faithfully give financial support to my international mission work, and keep me covered with prayer support. I thank God for the time he allowed me to be a part of Congregation Beth Hallel and to explore my Jewish roots.

GET AWAY FROM ICHABOD

"And she named the child Ichabod, saying The glory is departed from Israel: because the ark of God was taken, and because of her father in law and her husband." I Samuel 4: 21

"Don't use up your earth-time in a museum masquerading as a church. Find a place where the presence of God can be felt."

When I was in London several years ago, I had the privilege of visiting the British Museum. It was a fascinating place, and I left excited about the possibility of coming back. During the same stay in London I visited another "museum." It was the restored Metropolitan Tabernacle where the famous Charles Spurgeon preached several times per week. I had read much about Spurgeon's great ministry and dozens of his sermons. I looked forward to visiting the place where some of those mighty sermons were preached to crowds of thousands. I thought: this will be the highlight of my visit to London. But I left that place in a depressed mood.

In its heyday, 5000 people jammed into that auditorium for every service. My friends and I had the privilege of standing in the very pulpit where Spurgeon once stood. We noticed that our voices reverberated and magnified greatly in that cavernous hall. While standing there, I remarked that there was a gold-braid rope around the first two pews. The curator told us that those two seats were reserved for the congregation which still met there. Only about 30 people were currently attending the Sunday services. Where the fires of revival once brought packed crowds and attracted the attention of an entire nation, there was now a great sad emptiness. The glory had departed. That's not the only place like that. Visit the auditoriums of Yale, Princeton, Harvard and half a dozen other Ivy League schools. They all had their beginnings as centers of religious fervor. But now, you will find that where the excitement of revival preaching once dominated, today there is no interest in promoting Christianity at all. The glory has departed. God allowed me to see this to teach me a lesson. Each generation is accountable to God. We cannot live on past glory.

In the years that followed in my own ministry, I would be reminded of this lesson again and again. I remember great seasons of blessing in churches I have served over the years. Yet on occasional return visits, I often find that the glory has departed. Crowds have dwindled and the focus of the church has gone from outreach to maintenance status. But perhaps in the same neighborhood there is a younger church, and it has become the new hub of Christian activity. The glory we previously enjoyed has moved to a new location.

A friend of mine, Gerald Derstine, is the founder of Christian Retreat in Bradenton, Florida, and of a worldwide ministry. He has been particularly effective reaching Muslims for Christ in Israel. He once wrote a book called *Following the Fire*. Gerald had to move from his childhood religious background with the Mennonites to follow the fire of the Charismatic Revival. That's the idea. If you find yourself in a museum masquerading as a church, with a group of people more interested in the past than in the present, you need to move. Find where God is moving and follow the fire. That is where you and your family can grow spiritually, and where you can find a place of significant service.

Don't stay in a place dedicated to maintaining a memory of things that once were. That's Ichabod. Find where the glory resides now. Jesus is always on the move. If you want to stay near Him, you must be willing to move as well. Otherwise, you will settle for far less than your God-designed destiny. God forbid that you should settle down and spend your years in the foggy swamp of the depression called Ichabod. Do as my friend Gerald did: make it your life task to follow the fire of God's glory.

YOUR PAST IS NOT YOUR PROBLEM

"But the Lord said unto him, Go thy way: for he is a chosen vessel unto me, to bear my name before the Gentiles, and kings, and the children of Israel:" Acts 9: 15

"No matter what your past looks like, God can use you. God's grace is that big."

In this Scripture, Ananias is being told by the Lord to get over who Saul used to be. God says now he is a chosen vessel. He had a wicked past, but God can save him and clean him up and use him anyway. You may be struggling to understand how God could call you, of all people, into the Gospel ministry. Consider this: God uses people with a past. If He didn't, he wouldn't have anybody left to use at all! First of all, Calvary covers all your sin. Secondly, the Spirit of Christ in you is changing you into a new person. Thirdly, the grace of God is greater than your past.

In a jail when I was saved; I immediately felt the call of God on my life. For weeks I struggled; not against it, but trying to understand it. I was in no way qualified to be a minister of the Gospel. Although born again, I was still messed up emotionally and psychologically. I now had a criminal record. Being already extremely shy, and now ashamed of my past, I couldn't speak before groups. And of course I had little knowledge of God's Word. Eventually a pastor helped me understand on the basis of I Corinthians 1:26-29 that I didn't have to be qualified. God first chooses a vessel, then He prepares it.

John Newton, a former slave trader and drunkard, wrote the hymn, "Amazing Grace." He had a past. Another song writer, Haldor Lillenas, was thinking about his own past when he was inspired to write the hymn, "Wonderful Grace of Jesus." One of the lines in the chorus says, "Broader than the scope of my transgressions, Greater far than all my sin and shame, O magnify the precious name of Jesus, Praise His name!" I had a past when God called me into the ministry. I was saved in jail, and then immediately called of God to preach the Gospel. I constantly marvel at the grace of God that He would do such a thing. Yet by the amazing grace of God, I have preached the Gospel over 48 years.

Just look in the Bible! God uses people with a past. When God was looking for someone to be the first preacher of the good news that Jesus was risen from the grave, He chose Mary Magdalene. She had a past. Jesus had delivered her from seven demons. When God was looking a preacher at Pentecost, He chose Peter. Peter had a past. He had cursed and denied that he ever knew Jesus. When God was looking for a preacher to announce the good news of Christ to the village of Samaria, He chose the woman at the well. She had a past. Five broken marriages and shacking up when she met Jesus! When God was looking for someone to reach the ten city area of Decapolis, He chose a man who once was filled with a legion of demons. He had a past. When God was looking for the first great missionary to the Gentiles, He chose Saul, a killer of Christians. He had a past.

Your past is not your problem. Jesus looks at the mountain of sin in your past and disolves it all in a small pool of sinless blood at the foot of the Cross. If you have a problem answering the call of God on your life, it may be your lack of understanding the transforming power of the Spirit of Christ who has turned you into a new creation. Or, it may be your lack of understanding the grace of God. But there is a God-given faith now in your heart that can help you accept what you cannot understand. Trust the Lord as I have, and He will use you in spite of whatever past you have. Jesus is far more interested in your future than He is in your past. He cares much more about where you are going than where you have been. Start now and make a new beginning. Totally commit yourself to the call of Christ. Make today the first day of the rest of your life – a life completely yielded to the One who has decided to use you as a chosen vessel.

NO REGRETS AND NO LOOKING BACK

"And Jesus said unto him, No man, having put his hand to the plough, and looking back, is fit for the kingdom of God." Luke 10:62

"Walking straight means no looking back. You turn your back on some things forever when you start walking with Jesus."

In this verse Jesus uses a metaphor that few people in our modern culture can understand. It is about how a man makes a furrow in a field with an ox or a horse pulling a plow. When you take the handles of the plow and start the animal forward, you must focus on keeping the animal going in the right direction and on keeping the plow in the ground at the right angle. The first time I read this verse, I knew exactly what it meant, because I grew up on a farm when we still used a mule to pull a plow. When I was about 10, my father started training me to work with a mule and a turning plow. We had one field which was what was called "new ground." It was the last piece of land to be cleared of trees and still had roots and stumps in the ground which made plowing straight rows very difficult. But in early Spring, we had to lay off straight rows across the length of the field. Here is what my dad told me to do. On one side of the field I was to look across and fix my eyes steadfastly on a certain tree, and plow straight toward it without looking back.

With mule and plow in position for the first row, I got "Ol' Buck" started with a gentle slap of a plow line on his rump. The two plow lines I held ran through his harness and fastened to either side of a bit in his bridle. When I wanted to steer him left or right I would do so with a slight tug on one line or the other. I kept the mule going straight toward a certain dead tree on the far side. It was tough going, and I had to struggle to keep the plow steady because of occasional old tree roots. It was about all I could handle with the muscles of a boy my age. Finally, about a third of the way across the field, I thought I had better look back to see if the furrow was straight enough. It was. I kept going, feeling better about my new skill. Then I thought I would look again at that straight row I was making. But the second time I looked back, I saw with dismay that there was a very crooked place in the row. It was right where I had looked back the first time. And when I got to the end of the field, I stopped Ol' Buck with the "Whoa" command. As I was about to turn him back into the field with a "Gee" signal (right turn) I saw that now not one, but two crooked places were in the row. Each one was where I had looked back.

The "talking to" that I got from my dad made that experience stick in my memory the rest of my life. In fact, the first time I read this scripture, I immediately thought of my childhood experience one early Spring, trying to lay off straight rows in new ground. I understood it. Jesus puts us to work in His field. Once we leave the old life and put our hand to His plow, we must never look back, or we will make a sorry testimony. If we get distracted and look back, we will not be able to go straight. Such a person is not ready for the Kingdom of God. You may be tempted to look back with some inexplicable fondness for the life you once had. If you go back even temporarily to the old habits, the old crowd, or the old entertainments, you will find it a very disappointing experience. You are not who you used to be. The pleasures of sin no longer satisfy. And then when you turn back to Jesus, you will be so sad that you have disappointed Him, and also sad because you have ruined what would have been a good testimony. You will have a crooked place in your row – your Christian reputation.

The would-be disciple in this scripture only wanted to delay following Jesus just long enough to go home to say farewell. What Jesus said to him may at first seem harsh, but it is the truth. Perhaps He was warning this person that when he goes home, he will run into a test of his commitment. Maybe some there in his home will try to talk him out of it. The great lesson here is this: if you haven't made following Him the greatest priority of your life, something will always get in the way. Jesus laid down His life for us, going through all that horrible suffering on the cross to pay for our sins and to prove His love for us. We have decided to follow Jesus. We start on one side of the field of this life. We must plow a straight furrow to the end. Now we need to make very sure that nothing can make us look back. Whatever things have been tempting you, renounce them. They belong only in your past. The future in Christ is straight ahead - no regrets and no looking back.

IN THE PLAN, SON, IN THE PLAN

"And thine ears shall hear a word behind thee, saying, This is the way, walk ye in it, when ye turn to the right hand, and when ye turn to the left." Isaiah 30:21

"We have our plans, but God has the only plan that will work for our lives. We need to learn and listen to the voice of the Holy Spirit."

In the early 1970's, I was a guest speaker at a conference on the Holy Spirit in West Palm Beach. One of the guest speakers did not arrive, and just as the planners of the meeting were discussing what to do, an elderly man with a British accent walked up. He said, "Hello. I'm Arthur Burt from Chalk, England. God sent me here. Who's in charge?" When he told us how he got there, we all knew he was the replacement speaker. And oh, what an anointed message he brought. He spoke about "Staying in the Plan." God used him to touch and change the lives of many pastors that week. How did he get from Chalk to our conference in West Palm? God woke him in the middle of the night before and told him to go to the airport and get a ticket to New York. He got up and dressed and packed and left for the airport, although he had no money for the fare. The airport terminal was almost empty that late in the night. He sat down and closed his eyes and waited. Soon, he heard steps approaching him. A man said, "Sir, are you Arthur Burt?" "Yes," he answered. The stranger then took out of his pocket several hundred dollars and said, "Well, I don't understand this, but I know God woke me about midnight and told me to come here and give you money for a ticket to America!" Arthur took the money, bought the ticket, and flew to New York. From there, God further directed him to West Palm.

I was so impressed with Arthur's ability to hear God's voice, I wanted him to come and teach in the church I currently served: Woodlawn Baptist Church in Decatur, Georgia. I asked him if he could spare some time in the next year to come to Decatur. He smiled and said, "In the plan." I was pleased. I took out my planner notebook and asked what date would work best. The man of God just looked at me with a level gaze and said it again. "In the plan, son, in the plan." Suddenly, I got it. He was not about to commit to any plan until he had heard from God on it. That was a lesson I have never forgotten. It turned out shortly afterward that I left Woodlawn. Had I been able to engage Burt, we would have had to cancel the meeting. God knew the future and did not allow Burt to make that engagement. I never heard from Arthur Burt again, but I have remembered his words many times. "In the plan, son, in the plan."

God has the plan. We just have plans. In this word by Isaiah, our Father promises we will hear a word from Him, telling us which way to turn. And Proverbs 3:6 tells us that if we acknowledge Him in everything, He will direct our paths. What a wonderful way to live! Just following the Plan! But you may be wondering, "Why don't I hear God's voice like that?" Ask yourself two more questions: "If I heard God's voice, would I recognize it?" "If I knew it was God, would I obey without question and without hesitation?" The answer to both questions cannot be truly "Yes," or else you would hear God's voice more often. Pray to become sensitized to the leading of the Spirit, and to become flexible enough to change your plans at a moment's notice.

GOD PUTS YOU IN THE RIGHT PLACE AT THE RIGHT TIME

"And the angel of the Lord spake unto Philip, saying, Arise, and go toward the south unto the way that goeth down from Jerusalem unto Gaza, which is desert. And he arose and went: and behold, a man of Ethiopia, an eunuch of great authority under Candace queen of the Ethiopians, who had the charge of all her treasure, and had come to Jerusalem for to worship, Was returning, and sitting in his chariot read Esaias the prophet. Then the Spirit said unto Philip, Go near, and join thyself to this chariot." Acts 8:26-29

*"You may not understand why God directs you to a certain place,
but if you go there you will become part of a divine chain of events."*

Philip did not need to understand God's rationale for having him leave Samaria and go to a desert place. He just needed to obey. The entire city of Samaria was responding to
Philip's ministry. Suddenly he must leave and go a hundred
miles away to a deserted roadside and wait. Yet he obeyed the
Lord and did so. Very soon he saw a chariot approaching, and
God told him to intercept it. His being in the right place led to
the conversion of a high official of Ethiopia who would take
the Gospel back to his country. Few people understand how
precisely the Spirit of God can direct our steps. But God has
shown me several modern examples of ordering our steps just
as He did in this story of Philip and the Ethiopian. Let me
share with you one such story.

Peter Park was a pastor from Seoul, Korea. In 1981 he and
a group of pastors were praying and God directed them to
send one of their number to the United States. He was to go
and find someone to come and establish a seminary in Seoul.
They had 70 pastors desiring biblical and theological training,
but no instructors to teach them. Peter was selected to be sent,
although he spoke no English. Peter had relatives who had
settled earlier in Los Angeles, so he booked a flight from Seoul
to Los Angeles. Once he arrived in Los Angeles, however, he
was unable to contact his relatives. The phones numbers he

had were no longer in use. So, unable to speak English, Peter didn't know what to do next. As he prayed, the word "Atlanta" came to him. He felt led of God to go to an airline clerk and say that word. He did so, and got results. The clerk checked his identification, sold him a one-way ticket to Atlanta, and directed him to the gate. He had no idea where Atlanta was, but felt he must take the flight.

Of course no one greeted Peter when he arrived, and there was another time of prayer after he collected his luggage. He felt led to go to a phone book and look in it. Of course he could not read English, so he just scanned the yellow pages looking for Christian symbols such as a fish or a cross. He found an ad placed there by Our Shepherd's Church, which had a symbol of a cross and a dove. A passerby who could speak Korean helped him make a phone call to the church office. He wanted to meet the pastor. The secretary explained that the founding pastor had just resigned, but that he still lived in the area. She told him that her former pastor's name was Doug Chatham, and she gave him my phone number. Minutes later, I received a phone call from a Korean interpreter, who told me that a Korean pastor wanted to come out to my farm and visit with me. I wasn't feeling well, joints aching from the Lupus which had caused my resignation. I didn't really want company. I asked, "When does he want to come?" Peter Park's reply was relayed: "Right away. We can be there in about an hour." I was less than thrilled, but I said that would be fine, and gave them the difficult directions to my farm from the Atlanta airport.

Peter visited me, speaking through the interpreter. He told me that he believed God had sent him all the way from Seoul to my farm to get me to go back to Korea with him to help establish a seminary. I told him I thought he was mistaken, but I would pray about it. Peter went back to town to stay with a Korean family until I gave him my answer. I asked God for wisdom and I began to survey my situation. I was sick with Lupus, and might be a medical liability to the Koreans if I went in that condition. Besides that, I was out of work and my family had no income. Peter had promised that they would have excellent doctors for me in Korea, and would provide a good salary to help me support my family back in Georgia until I could move them. But my son Douglas was only 16, and needed to finish high school. I prayed and had no peace about going to Korea at this time in my life. My family needed me, and I needed my family.

What about that unique chain of events that brought a Korean pastor to my farm? I know God was in it. So if I was not the one to answer the "Macedonian Call" to Korea, who could it be? In that season of my life, I was related to a support network of ministers in South Georgia. I decided that I would take a three-hour ride with Peter to Jessup, the town where they would meet that Saturday. I told Peter that the other men of God would help us pray about the matter. When we got there and I shared the situation with them, one of the pastors began to weep. This pastor explained that God had been dealing with him for weeks about going as a missionary to South Korea. He knew this was God's doing. We were amazed. He had the academic credentials, he was from a theological background similar to Peter's group of pastors, and he and his wife had already agreed to answer God's call. Peter was elated! God led him to Los Angeles, then to Atlanta, then to me, and then through me to this pastors' meeting in Jessup, Georgia! And here he found the man God sent him to bring back to Korea.

My part in the whole thing was very small but important. Without my willingness to meet Peter, my willingness to pray about God's will for my life or my willingness to take Peter to the pastors' meeting, Peter's entire mission might have failed. God had a purpose for me to fulfill even when I was depressed and sick. How thankful I was to God that I had not missed that purpose. You may not understand why you are where you are at this moment, but God has a purpose for it. You are in the right place at the right time for the next step in God's plan for your life. Who knows what huge chain of events has already started – a chain of events that will eventually involve you? And who knows just how God will use you in that divinely-planned sequence? Stay tuned to the Spirit of God so that you won't miss your special moment when it comes.

GOD HAS SOME PEOPLE HE WANTS YOU TO MEET

"As soon as ye be come into the city, ye shall straightway find him, before he go up to the high place to eat: for the people will not eat until he come, because he doth bless the sacrifice; and afterwards they eat that be bidden. Now therefore get you up; for about this time ye shall find him." "Now the LORD had told Samuel in his ear a day before Saul came, saying, Tomorrow about this time I will send thee a man out of the land of Benjamin, and thou shalt anoint him to be captain over my people Israel, that he may save my people out of the hand of the Philistines: for I have looked upon my people, because their cry is come unto me." I Samuel 9:13, 15-16

"In God's plan for your life there are certain people placed at divinely-appointed intersections of time and space. Keeping such appointments will forever affect your destiny."

In this scripture passage, Saul is just out looking for some lost mules, but he finds a kingdom. God had so arranged his route that on the very day the prophet Samuel would be in a certain city, Saul would want to inquire about a meeting with him. All he thought he wanted from Samuel was a little insight as to where the mules might be. And in the meanwhile, God had already spoken to Samuel the day before that Saul would be there, and gave the prophet instructions concerning Saul. History would be made in that meeting. The first king over Israel would be chosen and anointed. Lives would be changed. We sometimes have encounters without realizing that we are keeping divinely arranged appointments. God has some people he wants us to meet.

In Jackson, Mississippi a college girl named Jackie felt in her spirit that God wanted her to marry a preacher. Then, in a strange turn of events, she transferred from her local four-year college to a junior college halfway across the state in the town of Newton. During her first week at the new college, she caught the eye of a ministerial student named Doug. That's how I met the lady who has been my wife and partner in the ministry for over 45 years! God had her transfer to my school so that we could meet and fall in love. We met at a divine intersection. We talk about coincidences. But really, once we learn how big God is, we have to know that they are not coincidences, but arrangements made by God!

Years ago, while I was serving as pastor in Milton, Florida, a group of pastors wanted to put on a county-wide evangelistic crusade. I was named as campaign chairman. We engaged a young Texas evangelist who flew himself and his minister of music in his own small plane to our local airport. He preached a wonderful crusade and I got to know him as a genuinely dedicated young man of God. His name was James Robinson. He would later have a nationwide television ministry. Years later as I read a book called, "The Faith of George W. Bush," I learned that in Texas, Robinson was the regular Bible teacher and mentor to a man who was about to become a two-term president of the United States! That book fell into my hand at just the time I was wondering if the stories about Bush's faith were true. I believe that God who knows the future arranged for me to know James Robinson personally so that years later I could have an answer when I needed it. Another divine intersection!

In 1970, a burning hunger for a deeper spiritual life led me to attend a series of meetings led by the late Vance Havner, a great Bible teacher during the middle of the twentieth century. He was speaking at the First Baptist Church of Milton, Florida He was saturated with the Word of God and he spoke with such authority and clarity that hundreds crowded the altars in every service. I met with him alone one afternoon and asked him to pray for me. He prayed a powerful prayer and I felt something change deep in my spirit. I remember him resting his hand on my head and praying that I would become a man filled with the Word of God. That moment permanently changed my style of ministry. It was a divine intersection.

Something like that happened in 1985 in Greer, South Carolina. My wife and I were invited to drive up from Conyers, Georgia to attend a hotel breakfast meeting with a group of pastors. George Otis of High Adventure was to be the speaker. During a break in the meeting, he approached us in a hallway and said he wanted to pray for us. God led him to pray for a release of financial blessing in our lives. We both knew it was from the Lord. We had not mentioned it to him, but we had been struggling for the past few years. I had just been healed from Lupus, but not before my medical bills and loss of income had taken their toll on our family. We left that encounter with happy hearts. We somehow knew God had turned it around. That's exactly what happened. Our income grew, debts were paid, and we began to have money to give to various ministries. We knew that meeting with George Otis was a divine appointment at a divine intersection.

The timing of some encounters is almost incredible. In July

of 1976 Jackie and I arrived at a booksellers convention in Atlantic City just as bookstore owner Bob Shirley and his wife Shirley were leaving. Just as they headed for the door, someone introduced them to us, since we also were from Atlanta. As we chatted briefly, they told me they were from the area of Mableton. I said that was an odd coincidence, since God had recently laid something on my heart about Mableton. I told them I was a church planter, and that I was being directed to help start a church in Mableton. Then came a startling bit of information: they then told me they had been praying for someone to come and use the back of their bookstore as a meeting place to start a full-gospel church. I said God had already shown me on a map the location where I was to plant a church, and that it could only be at the intersection of Bankhead Highway and Gordon Road Extension. They were stunned. That was exactly where their bookstore was located. That summer we launched a church and a Christian school in that bookstore. A divine appointment!

I could mention many other people whom I have met at those divine intersections over the years of my walk with Christ. Some of them were Lester Sumrall, Pat Robertson, John Edmund Haggai, Tim Hogg, Enoch Nascimento, and Jamie Buckingham. Each of them was used to shape my future. Sumrall and Robertson both interviewed me over their television networks. Haggai spoke in chapel at the New Orleans Seminary in 1968, and his missionary vision of training nationals became my model. Tim Hogg was a fellow pastor in Conyers who understood my call to teach ministers and urged me to apply at Beulah Heights Bible College where I have served ever since. Enoch Nascimento, vice-consul for the Brazilian government showed up in my classes as a student and has since helped open countless opportunities in Brazil and serves as my interpreter. I met Jamie Buckingham at a convention of Southern Baptists and he later wrote the introduction to my best seller, the *Rapture Book*. So many divine appointments. I can not possibly imagine how my life would have turned out without them.

My friends, believe me when I say this. God has some people He wants you to meet. And if you will just let Him have His way with you each day, you will meet them. In fact, you already have. You should thank God for the people He has used to shape your life and to bring you to this moment. Remember that like Philip, you may have to stop doing what you're doing and take a new direction in order to meet the next key person at the next divine intersection. If you're willing, God is willing.

TRANSIENT AMNESIA AND WASTED LIVES

"So teach us to number our days, that we may apply our hearts unto wisdom." Psalm 90:12

"The greatest loss is not inflicted upon us by one who steals our money, but by one who steals our time."

We should pray as Moses did here: ask the Lord to teach us to number our days, so that we can make wise use of them. Few of us are truly wealthy with money, but we all have more money than we have time. Money can be replaced. Time cannot. Therefore it is an even greater tragedy to waste time than to waste money. While I was being treated for Lupus, I was given two separate rest medications so that I could sleep at night. I didn't realize it at the time, but at the top of the list of possible side effects of each was transient amnesia. So they combined in effect to give me temporary amnesia, and I lost two weeks from my conscious memory.

During that time I appeared to function, although poorly. I spoke in a Bible study, but later I was told I had rambled so badly the people stayed after the service to hold a prayer vigil for me. I repaired a back porch but later thought my son must have done it since I didn't remember doing it. I dropped off a suit at some cleaning store, but have yet to discover which one. I remember nothing at all about that two-week period. It was a total loss. When I think about it, I feel deep sadness. I grieve for a part of my life I can never regain.

Our life on earth is too short as it is. We need to be redeeming the time – turning it into something that counts for eternity. "Redeeming the time" is a phrase from Ephesians 5:16. "Time" there is from the Greek word *kairos*. It means moment of opportunity. "Redeeming" is from the Greek word *exagorazo*, which means to buy out of, or to exchange for something more useful. Are you converting your time on earth to the currency of heaven?

Jesus taught that we are to lay up treasures in heaven that cannot be lost to thieves nor to the ravages of time such as rust or moths. You do that when you convert your time into eternal treasure through wise living. Moses said, "Teach us to number our days, that we may apply our hearts to wisdom." Paul told the Ephesians, "Wherefore be not unwise, but understanding what the will of the Lord is."

I wake up each day more and more excited that God has graced me with another day of opportunity. Do you? I am grieved when I see people waste their lives in idleness and worldly entertainments. Do you know that some people sit in front of TV sets so many hours per week that it actually adds up to years out of their lives? In a way, that's transient amnesia! In the words of Romans 13:11b, "...it is high time to awake out of sleep..." Let's start saying no to the temptations that trivialize our lives and eat up our time. Let's seek the will of God in every moment, and pack that moment to the full with memories we will treasure in eternity!

KEEP YOUR PROMISES

"Better is it that thou shouldest not vow, than that thou shouldest vow and not pay. Suffer not thy mouth to cause thy flesh to sin; neither say though before the angel, that it was an error: wherefore should God be angry at thy voice, and destroy the work of thine hands?" Ecclesiastes 5: 5-6

"A promise is no more trustworthy than the character of the per-

son who makes it. It is a reflection against your personal integrity if you do not keep your promises to others."

God intended that our earthly fathers be an example to our children of His faithfulness. One of the greatest sins a father can commit is to destroy his own trustworthiness in the eyes of his child. When my children were young, I often rewarded good behavior by promising a time of togetherness on some special occasion. It might be a picnic, a fishing trip, or a movie. Sometimes I promised my daughter Teresa that just the two of us would dine out at a restaurant and afterward help her do some shopping. How she enjoyed those "dates" with Dad. It would have been devastating to her trust in me if I had a habit of forgetting my promises.

My son and I also enjoyed special times away together. We camped in Stone Mountain Park, backpacked on the Jack River and the Chatuge River in the North Georgia mountains and hiked on the Appalachian Trail. I would promise that on a certain date, we could have one of these adventures together. Douglas Jr. would then happily make plans weeks or months in advance. How it would have hurt him if I had later broken my promise! But there were times when my poor planning resulted in calendar conflicts. I promised Douglas Jr. that we would go camping and boating on Lake Lanier on a certain weekend. We borrowed a boat and a tent and collected supplies. Then I remembered that I had committed to have a youth-led revival in our church on the same weekend. What to do? People expected the senior pastor to support the youth revival. But as I began to pray for wisdom, God showed me that my promise to my son took priority. I put other staff members in charge, and my son and I went ahead with our plans.

We set up our tent on a campsite in the park, put the boat in the water and cruised Lake Lanier, exploring all the inlets and the beautiful scenery. Late that evening we cooked out, and enjoyed sitting around our campfire about the same time that the youth services got underway. My son was amazed that I would leave the special weekend at the church to be out on the lake with him. To this day, he remembers how I kept my promise and put him ahead of my church duties. Our Heavenly Father is faithful to keep every one of His promises to us, His children. It grieves Him when we display a different spirit and by our broken promises abuse the confidence that people place in us. This scripture says it is better to not make a promise than to break it. Some of us have been hurt by broken promises. We still bear emotional scars. Let's pray and let God heal us as we remember that we also have hurt others through broken promises.

Over the years, God has worked this lesson into my character. "Always keep your promises. It is better not to make a promise than to make it and then break it." Our promise-keeping becomes our reputation of integrity. Our society seems to be afflicted with a generation of ministers who have yet to learn to make promise-keeping a priority. They promise to attend special meetings and then simply don't show up. In their own churches, they announce that a meeting will start at

7 PM, and they themselves don't arrive until 7:15 PM. Oddly, they seem perplexed that people in their congregations often make commitments and then fail to keep them. I believe the two things are linked spiritually. When ministers set the example and let their word always be truth, the people will learn to do likewise. Let's pray that people will find us more trustworthy.

CHURCH PLANTING IS "CUTTING EDGE" ADVENTURE

"And from Miletus he sent to Ephesus, and called the elders of the church. And when they were come to him, he said unto them, Ye know, from the first day that I came into Asia, after what manner I have been with you at all seasons," "And now, brethren, I commend you to God, and to the word of his grace, which is able to build you up, and to give you an inheritance among all them which are sanctified. I have coveted no man's silver, or gold, or apparel. Yea, ye yourselves know, that these hands have ministered unto my necessities, and to them that were with me." Acts 20:17-18, 32-34

"Few things equal the excitement I feel when I am planting a new church. It is costly to me and to my family, but it's always a great adventure. Church planters are on the cutting edge of the expanding Kingdom of God."

Paul here is reflecting back on his time of church planting

in Ephesus. It was a season of hard work and sacrifice. As he planted the church he had to provide his own income, working with his hands. He taught the whole Word of God from house to house for three years, and a great church was established. Some scholars estimate that at the time of this meeting between Paul and the elders of the church, there might have been as many as 100 cell groups, each with an elder in charge. It was a bittersweet time. He was seeing them for the last time, but he saw that a good church had resulted from the three years of service he had invested there.

My wife and I raised our children while we planted churches. We would begin regular Bible study with a small group – sometimes only two or three families. But God would send other workers, and we would always win many new souls who became part of our group. Two or three years later we would have a strong mission-minded congregation with its own property, meeting in a new building. At that point the church was able to provide a salary to fully support my family, but by then it was time to move on and start over. The soul-winning work on the "cutting edge" was exciting. The first few families that came to us in New Orleans helped us go to the French Quarter armed with gospel tracts and do street witnessing every Sunday night. Our church in Milton, Florida operated Destiny Theatre, an outdoor drive-in where you could take your family to see Billy Graham movies every weekend. Our Shepherd's Church of Stone Mountain often went on soul-winning excursions to such places at Little Five Points in Atlanta and to Underground Atlanta. Our children were important team players in these outreaches.

Those were precious years for my family. The children were quite small during the two years we planted Village d'Lest Church in New Orleans. But most of their formative years came during the eight years we were planting Our Shepherd's Church in Stone Mountain, Georgia. During that time we sent out church planting teams for successful plants in Mableton and Rex. Later, in only a few months I commuted to North Carolina and planted Evangel Fellowship in Spindale. What did we do for family income? Well, of course we became very thrifty, so we needed less than some families might. I was willing to work at other jobs as necessary, and God always honored our sacrifices with unexpected income. We stayed current with all bills, and all our needs were always met.

After the children were grown, I would spend another nine years establishing New Covenant Church in Covington, Georgia, and after that a few months starting Emmanuel Fellowship in Douglasville. But our most precious memories were those times when the children were young and our whole family was involved in the adventure of church planting. We often saw our needs miraculously provided. We would pray and God would answer. And that's how it was for the core group that faithfully helped us build. They saw daily miracles in their lives, too. The praise reports each week were invigorating.

The greatest thrill of it all was when people were saved and added to our church. Not many people may know this, but the most effective method of evangelism is church planting. Small, new, hard working churches grow primarily by getting lost people saved; and do a better job of follow-up. In New Orleans, we had a restaurant owner and Mafia member named Louis get saved. He joined our church and always sat on the front row in church. He didn't know our "spiritual" jargon. Instead of "Amen," he would often start clapping and say, "Bravo, Bravo!" On the cutting edge, there are lots of fresh responses to the Good News. Are you doing anything on the cutting edge? If not, it could be the reason your spiritual life is less exciting that it once was. Remember, someone was doing cutting edge work when they helped you find Christ! Let God put you back on the front lines. The thrill of adventure will keep you living on tiptoe!

NEW WINE IN THE OLD WINE FACTORY

"Others mocking said, These men are full of new wine." Acts 2:13

"It is often the case that unspiritual people are aware of changed behavior in new Christians but do not understand the cause. As you change, others may say demeaning things. But soon they will know better and acknowledge the reality of Christ in you."

What the mockers said on that first Pentecost was more true than they knew. The new wine of the Holy Spirit had been poured into human vessels. Jesus spoke about putting new wine into new vessels. Our lives must change, and ministry takes new form. Let me tell you about an unusual ministry in Mexico City. During the seventies, I made several trips per year to Mexico City to visit the ministry of a great missionary pioneer named Daniel Ost. Danny has gone on to be with the Lord now, but during his lifetime he and his wife Ruth founded a Bible College, raised up dozens of large evangelistic centers, and maintained a powerful radio and tract ministry. Totally immersing themselves in the culture of the people to whom God had sent them, they raised their children as Mexicans. Those children are all married to Mexican nationals and all are missionaries. Some remain in Mexico; others are in France and Spain.

Danny had a ministry vision with an unusual strategy. All around the perimeter of Mexico City, on major thoroughfares, he purchased old factory warehouses and theaters. One by one, he developed in each place a "Centro de Fe, Esperanza y Amor" (Center of Faith, Hope and Love). In front of each he erected a tall radio tower and at the top he placed a vertical sign proclaiming "Solo Jesus Salva" (Only Jesus Saves). Thousands crammed into these facilities to hear the Word of God. Each center could seat 3,000 to 5,000 people. And in each center, services were conducted all day long – 5 services per day. That was on Sunday. On other days of the week, at least two services were conducted daily. At the close of every service, about 20 lines were formed in front of as many counseling cubicles in the back of the facility. For at least a half hour after every service workers would be helping the altar call responders who stood in those lines.

What drew these large crowds? New wine! Against the backdrop of traditional religion in a Catholic country, Danny's ministry was fully Pentecostal. Miracles attended every service. People were healed of hopeless diseases. Demons came out of some. And Danny's workers saw that there was follow-up Bible teaching for every new convert. In the context of follow-up, many practical needs were also met in the love of Christ. On one occasion, I arrived late in the day from the US. The worker who picked me up had to make a stop by one of these centers before dropping me off at the hotel for much needed rest. As I waited for my driver, I stepped inside where one of those power encounter services was just letting out. In the crowd, someone spotted me as a visiting evangelist. Before I knew what had happened, a dozen people swarmed around me and someone guided my hand to the top of a boy's head. The boy, about eight, was on crutches and had a club foot. They wanted me to pray for his healing. I was tired and certainly did not feel very spiritual. But I did pray. Immediately the boy began to bounce around and dropped his crutches! He was healed! The people shouted and more people ran toward me – this time some coming from the street outside.

Suddenly, my hosts broke through the crowd and pulled me further inside the building. "Don't do it here," they pleaded. "Do it in one of the cubicles. The crowd is spilling out into the street and we will get in trouble with the police for blocking traffic. Please!" Tired as I was, I helped some workers in one of the booths pray for a long line of people, many of whom had missed the service, but came because of the commotion at the door. Incidentally, or maybe not so incidentally, the building had once been a wine warehouse. But it had new wine now! My only explanation to you is that it must have been the atmosphere of prayer and faith into which I had stepped. The power of God's Spirit was in that place. It wasn't me – that's for sure. But the experience showed me something.

Here was a man of God who didn't have to wait for a denominational hierarchy to decide if he could be a missionary. He had a calling, a vision and a passion. He committed himself to a city and began to win it to Christ. That's the kind of new wine we all need. How about you? Do you feel called to do something great for Christ? Have you been waiting for someone to give you an opportunity? What if you had to make your own opportunity? Pray for some of that spiritual new wine. I assure you that when you get it, you will find a new place to let it have its effect! God will see to that!

REBUKING A STORM

"Verily, verily, I say unto you, He that believeth on me, the works that I do shall he do also; and greater works than these shall he do; because I go unto my Father." John 14:12

"You can have authority over massive and awesomely powerful forces of nature. That is, you can if you are following instructions from Jesus."

There's no way that I could pretend to fully understand the verse we've just read. I believe it is true, because Jesus said it. But how? I have already experimented several times. I can tell you that there were times when I tried earnestly to do what Jesus did, in His name, and by His Spirit, and upon the authority of His written word; yet nothing happened. But there were times when I felt the Lord in me doing something miraculous and some wonderful thing happened. Perhaps you have had somewhat the same experience.

Let me tell you a story about an adventure I had in one of the early years that we were pioneering mission work in the Yucatan Peninsula. I traveled with a group of believers from one village we had recently evangelized to a more remote village that had never heard of Christ. Two other Americans were with me: Hayes Harper and Jerry McClelland. We went slowly by truck through the jungle and open henequen fields toward the village of Dzitzibalche. When we arrived at the village late in the day, we attracted a crowd – virtually everyone in the village. They watched as we began to set up a portable generator that we intended to use to show an evangelistic film in the open clearing. But strong winds began to whip through the thatched roofs and the palm trees. A dark cloud loomed on the horizon. Heavy drops began to fall.

It was the beginning of the monsoon season and the Maya Indians began to say knowingly that we were in for steady rain for hours. They thought we might as well get started making our way back to the first village while we still had a little light. But suddenly, a thought came to me so strongly that it seemed to be a voice. I heard it say, "Rebuke that storm." I had never thought of doing any such thing, so I hesitated. As I was hesitating, Jerry McClelland came over to me and said, "Brother, I believe the Lord is telling us to rebuke that storm." That did it. We stood together in the middle of the clearing and raised our hands up against the storm and said with loud voices, "We rebuke this wind in the name of Jesus Christ. Turn and go back where you came from."

Immediately the wind shifted and blew the storm back across the horizon, revealing a beautiful sunset! Four hundred pairs of eyes had witnessed the whole thing from the shelter of their huts. God had given them a mighty demonstration and opened their hearts to our message. We showed the film and preached and led dozens of souls to the Lord that evening. Workers were left behind to live with them and help them organize a church. There is a thriving church there today. Well, you can just imagine how empowered I felt then!

Two days later, we encountered another threatening storm. I felt equal to the task and said, "Watch this." I had some of the workers help me rebuke the storm. Nothing happened. A heavy rain ensued, and we were soaked to the bone! What made the difference? I heard no word from the Lord telling me to rebuke the storm. I learned a great lesson. I am still very pentecostal. I still believe in taking authority and binding the enemy. I still believe in rebuking the Devil. But I have learned that before you attempt to do some things which are contrary to nature, you had better check to see if in your spirit you have received orders from the Lord. There is a huge difference between obedience and arrogance.

Could this be the answer for you? If so, you can now be relieved of having to mimic some television stereotype. You don't have to put yourself and God's reputation on the spot unless you have something more solid to go on. Just learn to listen in every situation. There will be times you can only let nature take its course – even when destructive floods and storms strike. But you can also know that when it's the right time and the right place in God's plan, Jesus will give you authority to stop or turn a massive force of nature. When you get such a word in your spirit and God confirms it in the mouth of others, there will be an awesome display of God's power. He is a mighty God, and nothing is impossible for those who believe!

FINDING JESUS IN JAIL

"And at midnight Paul and Silas prayed, and sang praises unto God: and the prisoners heard them." Acts 16:25

"Sometimes good men go to jail so that bad men can hear God's word. And sometimes bad men are caught and put in jail so that they can later be some of God's good men."

The hundreds of men in the prison at Philippi had been arrested and put there for many different reasons. Some were drunks; some were runaway slaves, some were thieves; some were murderers. Only two were there because they were preachers of the Gospel: Paul and Silas. God allowed their arrest so that the bad men in that place could hear the gospel. God wants everyone to have one last chance. The prisoners heard a strange thing that night. They heard voices in the darkness praying and singing praises to God. They knew who it was. It was the same two men who had been beaten with many stripes, who had their feet locked in stocks in the inner dungeon. These men had open wounds; they were hungry and thirsty; they were weary; they were chained in an uncomfortable position; they were in a place that stunk with human waste. Yet they prayed and sang. Then there was that great earthquake that broke up the foundations of the prison. Doors popped open. The chains all broke. The prisoners were free. They could run away. But they did not. Why? They wanted to hear more about the God of Paul and Silas! They stayed, and we can suppose that many of them found Jesus. The whole thing was a set-up.

That's the way it was with me when I was a rebellious youth. I was living so recklessly that I was on my way to early death and eternal hell. I was put in the big Orleans Parish Prison just for one purpose: for one last chance to get the Gospel. Around me in that jail were hundreds of people, all arrested for various crimes There were thieves, drug dealers, murderers, drunks and junkies.. At first, I did not want to think I was like some of them. Other people had done some of the things that I had done. But I got caught and they did not. It was a set-up! I was a lost soul, and I was just as guilty before God as any of the inmates I saw around me. So God arranged my arrest. And He arranged for someone to give me a copy of the New Testament. I started reading it and discovered in Chapter Three of John how to be born again. It was the right time in my life and I was in the right place. I found Jesus. Rather, He found me.

Through my years in this college I have met many students who got started down the wrong road and wound up in jail, then met Jesus there and got on the right road. For others it didn't happen in jail, but God did send a big earthquake in their lives. And in their time of distress someone told them about Jesus. Thank God for the jails and the earthquakes! If weren't for those, many would never find Jesus. But Paul and Silas already knew Jesus. Why do you think they had to go to jail? For the other prisoners, for the jailer himself, and all his family. Paul practiced and taught the attitude that even bad things that happen to you can be for the "furtherance of the Gospel" (Philippians 1:12). So when they got arrested, he could look at Silas and say, "It's okay. God will use us in that prison." Paul was never a victim. He was a victor.

Is that the way it is with you? When you go through a bad time, do others hear you pray and praise God? Watch out! When you gripe and complain, others hear you! And it sends the message that your God can't help you in hard times. But when others can hear you can praise God in your darkest midnight, God has their full attention. Here is what we have learned in this passage. One, God uses your troubles to reveal Himself to you. Two, God uses your troubles to help you witness to others. Three, it's always midnight before God turns it around! But when He shows up, He puts on a show! Praise Him for all your midnights!

PREACHING IN BARS

"And he said unto them, Go ye into all the world, and preach the gospel to every creature." Mark 16:15, 20

"The early believers had in common one peculiar habit. They went everywhere preaching the gospel. They heard what Jesus said, and they went everywhere."

In our rush to take the Word to the ends of the earth, we often overlook pockets of unbelievers where we are, like those in jails and bars. We are concerned that there are lost souls on the other side of the world. So we raise thousands of dollars to make a quick trip to the other side of the world. It's full of adventure and excitement. But if it's lost souls we care about, then we can start closer to home with far less expense. I was saved in a jail. People in jail know they're not right with God. They know they have a fallen nature. They are already more afraid of hell than most folk raised in church. The gospel is good news to them.

I have found that people in bar rooms are also very responsive to the gospel. When I was a seminary student in New Orleans, I met Bob Harrington. At that time he was known as the "Chaplain of Bourbon Street." Bourbon Street was in the heart of the bar district of the French Quarter, famous all over the world for its "sin-holes." He introduced me to bar preaching. He took me with him several evenings to witness in the Quarter. Bob's ministry was in the streets of the most sinful part of the city of New Orleans. The only place in the Bible that I can think of, that was like the French Quarter was the city of Corinth. When Paul was in Corinth, he had a street ministry like Bob's. The streets in the French Quarter are lined with bars. In the late sixties when I was there, just to drive through the Quarter was to take a bath in filth. The doors of bars would be open to the street, loud music pouring forth, and nude performers easily seen by passersby.

Several bar owners knew Bob, and respected him as a person. They'd give him five or ten minutes to speak to everyone in their establishment. They knew he wasn't even going to make a dint in their business. He had a colorful way of speaking, and they probably thought he added to the entertainment. So one evening Bob took me into the most famous bar in America at the time – the Show Bar. The place was crowded, and there was a deafening din of noise. With a word from the owner, the scantily clad female performers took a break. The jazz band suddenly stopped. A piano player played on for a minute, then stopped. A hush fell over the bar. Bob introduced me, and I gave a five-minute testimony of how Jesus saved me and met the deepest needs of my life. The piano player and the band took up their instruments again. The performers came back on stage. But Bob and I sat a table and were thronged by weeping men and women who wanted to get their hearts right with God. We spent an hour praying with one after another. Several of them left when we left. They were through with that kind of life. They had found real happiness in Christ.

During the remainder of my time in New Orleans, I not only went to bars with Bob Harrington, but began to venture out on my own. Souls were always saved, where ever I went. Later I would hear from a few that they had started a new life and had joined a church. Only Heaven knows what happened to so many others. But they did hear the Gospel – even when they were hiding in a bar. It's strange how far we have drifted since the first century AD. Christianity, for many, is no longer a way of life; it is now a religion. It needs only be practiced in church or with other Christians. But Jesus told us to go every where preaching the Gospel. I think He still means it. You are here to join a new generation that will take Christianity back into the streets of the cities – even into the bars. As the saying goes, "You can run, but you can't hide."

What a relief to know that there are places to preach besides a pulpit. It is so frustrating to have such a powerful message bottled up inside and no place to preach it! Some students have come to me and said their denomination or pastor won't let them preach. So what! Jesus said you could go every where and preach! Let's pray that we will see and seize every one of the opportunities we are given. There is no higher calling than to simply testify for Jesus wherever you can. The enemy may have hoodwinked you by convincing you to wait until you get an invitation to preach in a pulpit. That's not how it was done in the New Testament. They just went everywhere talking about Jesus. It's that easy – once you love Jesus too much to quit talking about Him!

MAKING A COMMOTION FOR JESUS

"And hearing the multitude pass by, he asked what it meant. And they told him, that Jesus of Nazareth passeth by." "And as they departed from Jericho, a great multitude followed him. And, behold, two blind men sitting by the way side, when they heard that Jesus passed by, cried out, saying, Have mercy on us, O Lord, thou son of David." "And a great multitude spread their garments in the way; others cut down branches from the trees, and strawed them in the way. And the multitudes that went before, and that followed, cried, saying, Hosanna to the son of David: Blessed is he that cometh in the name of the Lord; Hosanna in the highest. And when he was come into Jerusalem, all the city was moved, saying, Who is this? And the multitude said, This is Jesus the prophet of Nazareth of Galilee." Luke 18:36-37; Matthew 20:29-30; 21:8-11

"Sometimes when you notice a crowd going somewhere, you might check it out. It could be about Jesus! And sometimes you ought to be the one to get the crowd going!"

Wherever Jesus went huge crowds followed. People asked, "What's going on?" Nothing stirs attention like an impromptu crowd. Street rallies and street marches are an effective way to draw attention to Jesus. I remember a youth revival in Milton, Florida in 1970. Our evangelist was Leo Humphries, who had a street ministry in New Orleans. We decided to have a "Jesus March." Early one morning about 200 youth rallied on the steps of Ferris Hill Baptist Church. Then with a brass band playing, and everyone singing, we started marching toward downtown. Leo carried a large cross up front. We caused a big commotion. People ran out into their yards to watch. Along the way we gave out tracts on how to be saved, and little red stickers that said, "I Love Jesus." As we crested a hill, two city workers crawled up out of a manhole and fell on their faces begging God to have mercy. They heard the music and saw the cross, and thought it was the end of the age. Dozens of people got saved that day. The commotion we made had eternal significance. And I learned something about doing ministry "outside the box" that has helped me ever since that time.

Have you made any commotions for Jesus lately? I mean, where outsiders can notice? The ministry of Jesus was not held inside church buildings like ours today. He walked the streets and roads, and His audience went with him. The ministry of Paul was not held in church buildings. He walked the streets of Philippi, and crowds followed him. Again, in the streets of Athens, crowds followed him. In Ephesus and in Jerusalem, crowds tried to mob him and kill him. Paul made a commotion about Jesus where ever he went. Are you that passionate about Jesus?

That's why I love the mission work that we do in developing nations. You don't have to get a permit to have an outdoor event. You just go to a park, or block off a street, and start singing and preaching. Crowds gather. People get excited. Something good must be happening, and they're afraid they will miss out on it if they don't hurry. We had a nightly crusade with about 25,000 people in Haiti without any promotion. We just had young people marching ahead of us playing trumpets, trombones and tubas. By the time we got to the site, the crowd was there. Recently we took a group of young people from our church on their first mission overseas. We went to sleepy little Mexican towns and started a commotion for Jesus. Here's what we did. Our youth would make balloon animals for kids. All the village kids came running. For the smaller children, the girls started some face painting. More kids came. So, some of the youth set up a puppet show with a Gospel theme. Adults came too. By that time it was dark and a crowd was there. Then we set up a portable generator and a video projector. We showed an evangelistic film and gave an invitation to Christ. Scores of children and adults committed their lives to Christ. Every night we started a commotion in a different town. And every night crowds came.

What's the secret to bringing crowds together? Not good "PR." You can spend and waste a ton of money on flyers and radio spots. But that's not what ignites excitement and interest. There's one secret element that works every time. What is it? Just pure, heartfelt passion. Passionate people find a way to express their passion. And passionate people always get your attention. So your heart burns to turn people on to your wonderful Lord and Savior? Then there's a way to make a commotion that will have people wanting to know more.

Think about it. Isn't there something you can do on weekends where you live to start a commotion outdoors? Or something indoors? What about starting with your friends and family. Get a Jesus video, or the Passion DVD, and host a viewing. Get all your neighbors to come to a get-acquainted block party. Don't allow any liquor or dope, but help everyone get high on Jesus. Or start a weekend "Jesus" art gallery display. Or put on a Christian music concert. Find a way to make people ask you, "What's going on!" When you get excited, people around you will get excited too. Start a commotion.

JUST FLASH YOUR HEADLIGHTS IF YOU WANT TO RECEIVE CHRIST

"Then he called for a light, and sprang in, and came trembling, and fell down before Paul and Silas, And brought them out, and said, Sirs, what must I do to be saved?" Acts 16: 29-30

"Folks can get saved anywhere, anytime. You just have to be ready to help them."

The jailer at Philippi wasn't waiting for daylight. Aftershocks from the earthquake were still shaking the ruins of his prison. He wanted to know how to be saved, and he wanted to know right then and there. Paul was probably still bleeding from a severe beating, filthy, tired and hungry. He could have said, "Help us get a good bath, some clean clothes and some food; and then we'll talk." Paul could have taken a "churchy" attitude and given the jailer an invitation to attend his services on the waterfront next Saturday. But his answer was, "Believe on the Lord Jesus Christ and you will be saved; and your family as well." And the jailer got saved there in the dark, and then took Paul and Silas to his house. There he cleaned their wounds, and they baptized him and his family. Then they had an early breakfast and rejoiced together as fellow believers.

This story reminds us that folk can get saved anywhere, anytime. You just have to be ready to help them. I have helped people receive Christ as their Saviour in hospital burn units, in funeral homes, in prisons, in bars, on street corners, and in private homes. Our church in New Orleans in the late sixties helped operate a coffee house for hippies. Every night 5 or 10 would come to Christ. Our church in Florida set up a full-sized outdoor drive in theater. We showed feature length films, usually from the Billy Graham Evangelistic Association. One that I remember was "The Cross and the Switchblade." There was usually a live performance by a Christian music group on stage at sunset. Then we showed one or two children's cartoons: Tom and Jerry, Daffy Duck, Bugs Bunny or Porky Pig. On Friday nights, lines of cars turned off the highway at our large lighted "Destiny Theater" sign, and drove down a lane between twin corridors of pine trees to the theatre area. There parking attendants helped get cars parked, and a concession stand did a lively business that paid for the cost of shipping the films.

Other churches pitched in with workers. At the end of each evangelistic film, someone took the stage and asked that no one start their cars just yet. Part of the condition for free admission was that they stay for ten minutes after the feature to hear a short presentation by the Theater chaplain. The families in the cars heard how to be saved, then the speaker would ask, "If you would like a Christian worker to come to your car and pray with you, just flash your lights!" And each time, we could see several sets of flashing headlights. There would be a time of prayer at the car, and then the family would drive away with a packet of follow-up material and directions to a participating church. Each summer, dozens of families were brought into our church through this novel outreach. It just points again to the fact that people can get saved anywhere. Our biggest challenge today, with so many church buildings available, is to think outside the box. Many people just will not come to your church until they are saved. Are you ready to meet them where they are?

There are workers out there on the highway driving eighteen-wheeler rigs that double as mobile chapels. The work is overwhelming and they beg for helpers. Others take special trailers and set up at motorcycle races to provide hospitality and a Christian witness. They need help. In dozens of prisons and jails in this city, there are prisoners waiting for someone to tell them how to be saved. Homeless shelters, AIDS hospices, and soup kitchens are filled with people who need someone to lead them to Christ. They won't or can't come to your church. But you can go to them! Let's pray and find a way to take the good news of Jesus to where they are. All things are done through prayer. If you pray for this open door, it will happen.

Pray that you will be in the right place at the right time for God to use you to show someone the Way. Pray that God will show you a way to serve. You don't have to wait until you have a pulpit. That may not be God's plan. But He does have a plan. When you find it, there will be hungry souls waiting.

"DADDY, I WANT TO GET SAVED."

"And Jesus called a little child unto him, and set him in the midst of them, and said, Verily I say unto you, Except ye be converted, and become as little children, ye shall not enter into the kingdom of heaven. Whosoever therefore shall humble himself as this little child, the same is greatest in the kingdom of heaven. And whoso shall receive one such little child in my name receiveth me. But whoso shall offend one of these little ones which believe in me, it were better for him that a millstone were hanged about his neck, and that he were drowned in the depth of the sea." Matthew 18:2-6

"Never stand in the way of children who want to come to Jesus. We must all come as children or not come at all."

Do you ever wonder how you could even be saved? I have, many times. But then I realize that on my best day, I am still just a child spiritually. Some current teaching fads may lead our church people to think that they are spiritual giants, when in fact they ought to see themselves as little children before the Lord. Let me share something personal with you. While I was pastoring in New Orleans, I noticed that my eight-year old daughter Teresa became very tearful and heavy-hearted during every service. In those days we were just getting a new church started and I preached a salvation message in almost every service. As she heard about what Jesus did on the cross for our sins, about being saved from hell when we die, Teresa felt the pull of the Holy Spirit on her heart. But at first, I couldn't imagine why she was crying. My wife Jackie told me, "She wants to be saved."

We sat down and talked, and then prayed with Teresa. Then she prayed aloud herself: a simple but heartfelt prayer, giving her heart and life to Jesus. She asked Jesus to forgive her for being a sinner. That was the hard part for me to understand. She was a normal child, with the usual mild streaks of misbehavior, but I had never thought of my sweet little girl as being a lost sinner. I wondered briefly if she really understood what it was to be a sinner. I talked with her and became fully assured that she knew exactly what she was doing. In the next service, during the altar invitation she came and I helped her tell the people that she had given her heart to Jesus and wanted to be baptized. That was the beginning of her Christian life.

Two years later, while I served a church in Milton, Florida, my son Douglas gave his heart to Jesus at the age of five. One night on the way to the home of some friends following a revival service, he leaned forward from the back seat and announced to us, "I want to be saved." "Good," I said, "That's great! When we get home we'll help you pray and receive Jesus in your heart." He said, "No, Daddy. I mean I want to be saved right now." There was nothing to do but to pull the car over on the side of the highway and let him pray with us right then. Little Douglas prayed a simple, straightforward prayer. "Dear Jesus, I want you to be my Saviour. I want to be a Christian. Please save me. Forgive me of all my sins. Thank you, dear Jesus. Amen." And as soon as he had said those words, he was visibly relieved. He was satisfied that the Lord had heard him and that he was saved. We could then restart the car and go on to visit with our friends. As we arrived, his first words to the young boy who lived there were, "I just gave my heart to Jesus!" It was my privilege to baptize both my children while they were yet very young. Why not? From the moment they consciously gave themselves to the Lord, I saw their attitude and character begin to become more Christlike. If their inner character had become more selfish, I might have had occasion to delay their baptisms. But they became less selfish, more kind and sweet in their nature. Both of them have been committed Christians ever since.

My children have taught me something. Jesus commanded us to let little children come to Him. What's more, He said we adults have to be converted and become like little children ourselves. What does that mean? Several things. First, it means we have to come with a childlike faith. It is not necessary to learn all the great Christian doctrines first. Who then could be saved? Second, we need to believe in Him the same way a child does. We just need to believe the simple Gospel message and give our hearts to Jesus. To a child, giving your heart to Jesus is telling Him you love Him and you want Him to be your special friend. A child can experience the release of forgiveness of sins just as easily as they can enjoy being forgiven by parents about something for which they expected to be punished severely. Third, it means that we have to come in humility. To a little child, parents know everything. If they can know so much, how much more would Jesus know all about us. So when we come to Jesus, we make no excuses for ourselves. We humbly beg for forgiveness.

That's it! We must all come to Jesus like children. What arrogance it is then, to demand that children be put off until they are older. One of the greatest ways to grow a church is to have a strong children's ministry. One of the greatest ways for you to serve in personal evangelism is for you to share Christ with children. Think about it: which is better? To come to Jesus at age 7 and live 70 more years serving Jesus – or to come to Jesus at age 70 and then live only 7 more years for Christ before you die? How wonderful it is to lead children to the Lord, and how wonderful it is for us to keep our childlike trust. How about you? Do you see yourself as a spiritual giant, or as a little child in the Kingdom of God?

WE HAVE A JOB TO DO

"Always bearing about in the body the dying of the Lord Jesus, that the life also of Jesus might be made manifest in our body. For we which live are always delivered unto death for Jesus' sake, that the life also of Jesus might be made manifest in our mortal flesh." 2 Corinthians 4:10-11

"We have a job to do that is so important we should let nothing stop us. My passion to preach is so strong that I have actually unknowingly preached through a heart attack."

Paul, in 2 Corinthians 4, gives us a picture of what it is like to be totally sold out to Christ. For him no obstacle or affliction was important enough to deter his ministry of the Gospel of Christ. In verses 10 and 11 he gives the basic principle that should characterize the life of every man or woman of God. It is what Jesus taught and demonstrated: dying to live. We must allow death to work in our physical bodies so that the life of Jesus can be manifest in our lives for others to see.

On Saturday, November 6, 2004, I experienced a heart attack while doing yard work. I found myself having difficulty breathing because of sharp pains in my chest. Unfortunately, I did not realize that the pain in my chest was really a heart attack. Since I have suffered many years from mixed connective tissue disease (MCT) which causes inflammations in various parts of the body, I assumed that this was another chest inflammation like those I had in the past.

On the morning of Sunday, November 7 I awakened early with a sore chest and shortness of breath. But that day was a great day for me. I was to preach the morning message at West Metro Church of God. Much more than my physical heart hurt, my spiritual heart was burning with God's Word. I made my way to the church where the elders met with me and prayed a powerful prayer for the anointing of God. When I stepped into the pulpit, I felt no pain and no shortness of breath. I knew the Holy Spirit was helping me, and so did the church. I preached from Romans 8:28 and shared several personal testimonies about how God always turns bad things around for those of us who trust Him. God used that message. People are still listening to and sharing copies of the tape.

That afternoon the pain returned and increased over the next several days. I tried to see a doctor in my HMO system, but the earliest I could see one was on Monday, November 15. By then I knew I was in trouble, and thought it might be something I had before: pericarditis, an inflammation in the lining of the heart. But the doctor, a Rheumatology specialist, was overbooked and in his hurry misdiagnosed my problem as stress related to sleep deprivation. He gave me some rest medicine and sent me back to work. I continued with my daily work schedule, but got weaker by the day. At night when I tried to lie down in bed, the pain became so intense that I spent two nights just sitting up in a chair.

Finally through the persistence of my wife Jackie, my personal doctor had an opening on Thursday, November 18. As soon as he saw the ECG results, his face became sad and he told me that I had suffered a heart attack. I was rushed direct-ly to the emergency room at Northside Hospital. By then, the tissue on one side of my heart was so badly affected that bypasses were out of the question. However, my church fam-ily, my college family, my many missionary friends, and pas-tor friends joined in a mighty concert of prayer, and God began to turn things around. I was moved to Saint Joseph's Hospital and there I underwent operations on two successive days. Through angioplasty, three stints were inserted which opened up enough blood flow to stop the pain and help me regain strength.

God has brought me back from certain death to walk in new spiritual victory. There was never any fear of death through the entire experience. As He says in His Word, I am bearing in my body the dying of the Lord Jesus so that the life of Jesus might be also made manifest in my body. After Jesus had died for our sins on the cross and conquered death for all time, He rose again to be the Life within every believer. Because of that Life, I found myself sharing Christ with all those around me – in the operating room, in the hospital bed, in the ambulance. And they listened. Nurses confessed that they were drawn back to my room because of the peace of the Lord they felt there.

We all have a job to do. You and I are called to proclaim the Word of the Lord in the power of the Life of Jesus. Sooner or later, you will face a choice of giving up or going on. But the more we minister through pain and weakness, the more others will feel the reality of Jesus. Therefore when pain comes, let it be a wake-up call. You have a job to do.